To Carl

AGILE CONSTRUCTION
FOR THE
ELECTRICAL
CONTRACTOR

P9-DBY-062

Dr. Perry Daneshgari

President and CEO
MCA, Inc.
Flint, Michigan

JONES AND BARTLETT PUBLISHERS
Sudbury, Massachusetts
BOSTON   TORONTO   LONDON   SINGAPORE

World Headquarters

Jones and Bartlett Publishers
40 Tall Pine Drive
Sudbury, MA 01776
978-443-5000
info@jbpub.com
www.jbpub.com

Jones and Bartlett Publishers
Canada
6339 Ormindale Way
Mississauga, Ontario L5V 1J2
Canada

Jones and Bartlett Publishers
International
Barb House, Barb Mews
London W6 7PA
United Kingdom

Jones and Bartlett's books and products are available through most bookstores and online booksellers. To contact Jones and Bartlett Publishers directly, call 800-832-0034, fax 978-443-8000, or visit our website, www.jbpub.com.

Substantial discounts on bulk quantities of Jones and Bartlett's publications are available to corporations, professional associations, and other qualified organizations. For details and specific discount information, contact the special sales department at Jones and Bartlett via the above contact information or send an email to specialsales@jbpub.com.

Production Credits

Chief Executive Officer: Clayton Jones
Chief Operating Officer: Don W. Jones, Jr.
President, Higher Education and Professional
 Publishing: Robert W. Holland, Jr.
V.P., Sales: William J. Kane
V.P., Design and Production: Anne Spencer
V.P., Manufacturing and Inventory
 Control: Therese Connell
Publisher: Kimberly Brophy
Acquisitions Editor, Electrical: Martin Schumacher
Associate Editor: Laura Burns
Production Manager: Jenny L. Corriveau
Director, Public Safety Group: Matthew Maniscalco
Associate Marketing Manager: Meagan Norlund
Composition: Cape Cod Compositors, Inc.
Cover Design: Scott Moden

Text Design: Anne Spencer
Assistant Photo Researcher: Meghan Hayes
Cover Image: (front cover, top image: © Kodym/
 Dreamstime.com); (front cover, middle row,
 left to right: © Lisa F. Young/ShutterStock, Inc.;
 © Patrick Hal/Dreamstime.com; Courtesy of
 Perry Daneshgari); (front cover, bottom image:
 Courtesy of Perry Danesghari) (back cover, left
 to right: © Rolf Klebsattel/Dreamstime.com;
 © ckflrbq/ShutterStock, Inc.; © Dmitriy
 Shironosov/ShutterStock, Inc.)
Part Opener Image: © Joe Gough/Shutterstock, Inc.
Chapter Opener Image: © Andreas Guskos/
 Shutterstock, Inc.
Printing and Binding: Malloy Lithographing
Cover Printing: Malloy Lithographing

Unless otherwise indicated, all photographs and illustrations are under copyright of Jones and Bartlett Publishers, LLC, or have been provided by the author.

Library of Congress Cataloging-in-Publication Data
Daneshgari, Parviz.
Agile construction for the electrical contractor / Perry Daneshgari.
 p. cm.
 ISBN-13: 978-0-7637-6562-0 (pbk.)
 ISBN-10: 0-7637-6562-7 (pbk.)
 1. Electric contracting. 2. Buildings—Electric equipment. 3. Construction industry—Planning. I. Title.
 HD9716.E432D36 2009
 621.319'240684—dc22

 2009018875

6048
Printed in the United States of America
13 12 11 10 09   10 9 8 7 6 5 4 3 2 1

Contents

■ Part III **Strategy for Agile**   139

Preface

Why are some companies profitable while others are not? Why do certain projects make money while others don't? For that matter, how can the world population grow from less than one billion in 1800 to more than 6.7 billion in 2008 with a higher per capita income and output than in the years preceding the Industrial Revolution? The Malthusian Trap, named after economist Thomas Malthus, was broken by improved human productivity. Once people were able to produce more than they consumed, through the increased productivity that followed the Industrial Revolution, they were able to enjoy a better life. The Industrial Revolution marked a major improvement in human productivity. With increased industrial productivity, we inherited a new and complex way of managing the resources necessary to accomplish work.

The improvement of productivity and innovation in construction companies is no longer just a result of using efficient tools. The distinction between a good contractor and an ineffective one depends upon how well each contractor manages his or her resources. Innovation in contracting now happens primarily in the process designs.

Nearly everything around us that we see, feel, and use has been designed and developed by a human. And most things are now designed for use in an optimal way. We expect a drill motor to help us drill a hole or drive a screw, and it does. We expect a bender to bend pipes, and it does. When it comes to processes, however, we often expect them to happen by themselves.

Agile Construction™ is an engineered process designed to respond to the owner's and general contractors' specific needs to become more efficient, more productive, and, ultimately, more profitable. Time, cost, and quality are the focus of the Agile Construction process design.

Agile Construction exemplifies the following characteristics: Visibility, Responsiveness, Productivity, and Profitability.

The purpose of this book is to examine the lessons learned from other industries that underwent a transformation to become more productive, and to understand how such change translated into success. The steps necessary to design and manage an Agile Construction company are described and explained herein.

Acknowledgments

I have had the good luck of being a lifelong student of many great men and women in my life. It is very hard for me to point out only one or two individuals who have influenced my life and professional education the most. Great men and leaders, such as Skip Perley of Thompson Electric; Robert and Jay Bruce of Bruce and Merrilees; Ted and Kent Baker of Baker Electric; Mike Holmes and Mike Richards of Holmes Electric; Jimmy Cleveland of Cleveland Electric; Gene Dennis; Russ Alessi, President of Electri International; Ed Hill, President of IBEW; Mark Ayers, President of the Building Construction Trade of AFL-CIO; Angelo Veanes of Ferguson Electric; Dick Pieper of Pieper Power; Ron Autrey from Miller Electric; Robert Reynolds, Dick Offenbacher, Arnold Kelly and David Moeller of Graybar Electric; David Los and David Crumrine of Interstates Electric; and countless others have all contributed to this book through the insights they have shared with me regarding the electrical construction industry. The real practitioners, such as Kim Mazuk, Ed Hillman, and Greg Sherman of Holmes Electric, Jerry Greeson and Ron Cook of Cleveland Electric, and many more taught me what it means to apply the theory of Agile Construction™ to real life. National Electrical Contractors Association (NECA) and local managers, the unsung heroes of the industry, such as Roger Simonds and Eric Sivertsen of the Northern New Jersey chapter of NECA; Tim Gauthier of the Oregon chapter; Bill Belforte of the Illinois chapter; Steve Allred of the West Virginia chapter; as well as Don Fiore and Jack Gilday of Long Island, New York have shown me how to win both management and labor support to achieve improved and lasting productivity.

My editors and publishers, Martin Schumacher, Laura Burns, and her predecessor, Lindsay Murdock, were a godsend to put up with my quirks.

Without the help of my companions, coworkers, and friends at MCA, Inc., I would not have had a prayer in collecting, compiling, analyzing, and presenting this work. Heather Moore began working with me over six years ago. She has helped me to avoid putting my foot in my mouth on more than a few occasions. Most, if not all, of the data, measurements, illustrations, and analysis in this book are her work. She is now working on her PhD in construction management. Look out for her, as she will change the industry. Heather has helped me write and develop the ASTM standard for productivity measurement. She has a mission in her life, and that is to help the construction industry be more productive. I am not sure how I got lucky enough to have such a brilliant person working with me.

Phil Nimmo conducted many of the onsite implementations and dealings with contractors done in preparation for the writing of this book. His work over the past eighteen years has helped companies to realize millions of dollars in profitability. Most contractors have improved their profits by more than 30 percent within a year after working with Phil. Phil's contributions can be seen throughout this book.

Anna VanWagner's patient work and follow-up kept everyone on schedule. She has worked with me for more than seven years and has not missed a beat while keeping me on task, which is no small feat.

Chantelle Jablonski has helped me for more than fourteen years in all aspects of research and presentation. Without her, this book would not have been assembled.

Naturally, you will see Michelle Wilson's work in this book. It is her tenacity and hard work decoding and analyzing data and applications that brings these intangible ideas to the tangible world. Her keen eye and ability to translate dry statistics into real-life applications are unmatched by anyone I know.

Like any writer who needs an outside mentor, without the support of my wife, Jennifer Daneshgari, JD, I would have neither the patience, the wit, nor the financial wherewithal to do my research for this book in addition to the other work I do for the industry. I am forever grateful and in debt for her love and graciousness.

Of course, you, the reader, are the most important part of this equation: Without you there can be no true application of Agile Construction theory. So please: relax, read, and execute.

—Dr. Perry Daneshgari

Introduction

Agile Construction™ is profitable construction.

Construction is a risky business. As an electrical contractor, you have to know everything about what it takes to bid a job, put it in place, and collect for it. You need to know how to bid a job and how to put the final prices together, and be willing to risk losing your entire life's savings on only one bad job. You have to know about electricians' jobs even though you may not be an electrician. You have to schmooze with general contractors (GCs) and put up with construction managers (CMs). You have to pay everyone who shows up to work, whether the work is productive or not. You have to give constant attention to every change on the job site, manpower, money, and material. You have to know how to deal with banks, insurance companies, and surety companies. You have to know about human resources and Equal Employment Opportunity Commission regulations. You have to solve everyone's problems and make all this happen in the safest way possible. If you do all of this right, you might even get paid.

Presence of mind and always being at the top of your game are basic requirements of being a contractor. These characteristics represent your agility, which allows you to respond to the constant requirements of your company. For your *company* to be agile, each of its processes and procedures must allow quick response to every requirement of the job. The company needs to develop the ability to respond to all the issues the same way that you do, based on your own experience. For this to happen, the company's activities must become visible, measurable, and traceable.

Recently, Lean Construction has been celebrated as the new fad in construction management. In reality, it is not the leanness of the construction that matters, but rather its agility and responsiveness to change. Agile Construction—a method of being responsive to the constantly changing environment and conditions of the job site that results from making job processes visible, manageable, and measurable—puts you in a position to react appropriately to the constantly changing job site so that you can stay ahead of the curve.

A construction job site is a fluid work environment, existing in a state of constant change, both planned and unplanned. Schedules change. Customer needs and requirements change, often frequently. Resources and experience levels change through ongoing familiarity with the job and again with every personnel reassignment. To be an Agile Construction company, every aspect of the company needs to work together as a synchronized machine. The entire company has to be Agile.

Agile Construction is a response to the needs of and input from both the job site and the company. It is a process designed and developed to help you achieve optimal responsiveness to the changing needs of the job site. Agile Construction starts with the customer and works back through the entire construction process. It provides the customer with a fully designed and installed project at the lowest overall cost to the contractor. An Agile operation applies managerial science to the three Ms—money, material, and manpower—to produce the highest quality product at the lowest cost and in the shortest time.

The cost of construction continually increases. At the heart of high construction costs is labor productivity, or the lack thereof. By applying management principles learned from other industries, the construction industry can improve labor productivity through improved system productivity, which is the productivity of the entire job. You must know how much of the labor's time was used for installation and how much of it was wasted. The ratio of the useful (installation-related work) hours to the total hours used is the productivity of the system. Agile Construction is the direct application of parallel managerial techniques such as Lean Engineering, Total Quality Management (TQM), Six Sigma, and other practices that have proved to reduce costs and risks in other industries.

This book shows you the tools, processes, and steps to become an Agile Construction company so that you can stay ahead of your competitors. This book:

- Identifies what *Agile* means in construction
- Explains the Agile principles and concepts as they apply to electrical construction
- Introduces the methodologies and tools that promote aspects of agility
- Develops the tools and processes for implementing agility in electrical contracting:
  - Measure and improve labor productivity
  - Enhance material management
  - Articulate and manage Short-Interval Scheduling (SIS™)
  - Evaluate and improve multivariable forecasting for estimation
  - Improve the financial predictability of the project outcomes
- Shows applied case studies and examples

Agile Construction is a journey. It requires understanding, commitment, and concerted effort. The dividends of agility—increased productivity and increased profitability—derive from the visible, manageable, and low-risk system that is Agile Construction.

This book is based on more than 20 years of work by MCA, Inc., in close collaboration with many progressive contractors. MCA, a research and implementation company that focuses on improving the productivity and profitability of the nation's construction industry, gathered the data and conducted the research.

What Is Agile Construction?

Agile Construction™ exemplifies the following characteristics:

- Visibility
- Responsiveness
- Productivity
- Profitability

Agility allows us to identify, address, and respond proactively and efficiently to the changing needs of the job site. True agility requires careful management of every window of opportunity, every gap between one event and the next.

Construction job sites have many "fires," "emergencies," and "urgent situations," no matter what they happen to be called. Every one of these events requires a certain amount of time to be identified as an emergency (time to detect) and a certain amount of time to formulate and implement a response (time to correct).

According to system design principles, time to detect and time to correct are inversely related. In other words, the longer it takes to identify a problem, the less time there is available to formulate and implement an appropriate response, and the more likely the response will be a costly emergency. The earlier you recognize a situation, the more time you have available to correct it. **FIGURE 1–1** shows this relationship.

Agility enables the contractor to be aware of the potential fires and to identify them as soon as feasibly possible to minimize the negative impact while taking advantage of the opportunities available. By understanding the relationship between the time to detect and the time to correct, we can avoid the firefighting situation.

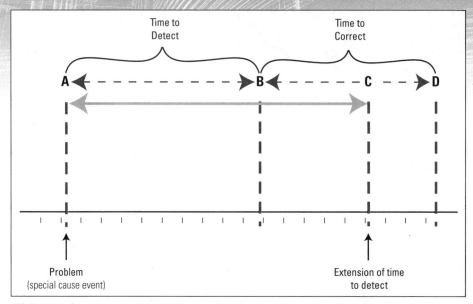

FIGURE 1–1 Components of response time.

Consider the following scenario: Suppose you plan to pull wire in area 2 (the west wing) of your job site on Wednesday morning. Everything is mobilized and everyone shows up at 7:00 a.m. to pull the wire; however, the report that morning from the GC says that you cannot start in area 2 because the mechanical contractors are still working in that location. Okay, no problem, you have run into this before; your employees can work in area 3 (the control room) instead. You demobilize and set up again in area 3, only to find that you don't have all the material you need. Because you have to follow the company's strict material ordering rules, you have to wait two hours for the supplies you need to get the job started in the control room.

By not being fully aware of the details of the situation, you are not able to respond effectively to the change in area. The time and effort spent waiting and demobilizing and remobilizing is wasted and results from poor system design and a lack of agility. However, you can't just change the material ordering process solely to respond to emergencies like this.

With an Agile system, you can proactively anticipate the needs through a visible system that brings in timely information. Could you have seen that the mechanical contractors were working with only half a crew the day before or had run into other unexpected delays? Could you have checked the location or the access or the materials the night before? Could you have asked the GC ahead of time? Could you have the material on site not only for the planned work, but for a contingency plan and an alternate as well?

With Agile tools and processes, the electrical contractor can put a system in place to identify issues such as this as quickly as possible so that he has the maximum possible amount of time to respond to them—lowering costs and increasing productivity in the process.

Consider the following:

1. If the material for the contingency plan of working in area 3 was already on site, you could have used the two hours of wait during the ordering process for installation.
2. If the GC kept a joint schedule with real-time progress measurements from all subcontractors that was available to all, you would have known that the area would not be ready and you would not have spent the time mobilizing that area in the first place. You could have spent the time mobilizing and demobilizing more effectively.
3. If the foreman or superintendent had checked the area ahead of time, that person could have known that the area would not be ready and could have put in material requests for the next area so that material was on hand in the new area as needed.
4. If there was communication between the subs on the job about their expected plans and schedules, as well as their historical ability to accomplish their plan and typical impediments, you could have potentially anticipated the non-completion of the area and made alternative arrangements to utilize the labor on the job site fully and effectively.

Agile Construction can help the contractor be more profitable though visibility, responsiveness, and increased productivity. Less time spent on nonproductive activities leaves more time for installation and reduces costs of installation.

Productivity and Production

Agile Construction™ provides the tools and information that allow the electrical contractor to increase system productivity. Before applying the tools, you need to understand system productivity. This chapter first investigates the difference between production and productivity and then the difference between individual productivity and system productivity.

■ Production

In construction, production is what has been done—installation or fabrication. Therefore, production in construction is defined by construction-put-in-place (CPIP) in any shape and form of installation or prefabrication, which can be measured physically by walking through the job site and observing the progress of the project. You can also measure production from the accounting perspective through earned revenues based on current incurred cost, which shows the proportion of the cost to date as the percentage of the estimated total cost.

■ Productivity

Productivity, on the other hand, is the effectiveness of production. How effective was the labor in production installation? Productivity can go up or go down in relation to the base line for measurement. Correct measurement of productivity is a fundamental cornerstone of Agile Construction.

The productivity of the labor in Agile Construction is measured by the time the labor spends on the installation or any other value-added activities versus the total time spent on the job. In other words, Agile productivity is the ratio of useful hours to total hours.

The company uses assumed productivity to create the labor units for installation. Base line productivity is based on the assumption made by the estimator about the labor hours needed for various installations. If the labor performs better than the base labor units suggest, then the labor is more productive. If the labor takes more time, the labor is less productive. Base labor units, which are the allocated labor hours per take-off item, whether factored (adjusted) or unfactored (unadjusted), typically come from historical average labor performance, which includes all the nonproductive and wasted hours.

Even the hardest worker, trying his or her best to get things done, often finds that work on the job site just doesn't go the way it should. Despite the fact that the worker just spent an 8- or 10-hour shift working on the job site, the project is no closer to completion and could even be further away. For example, a crew may spend several days preparing for power on the seventh floor. A new power generator is delivered to its permanent home in the subbasement—the plans have changed and a power room is no longer needed on the seventh floor. Now, the general contractor (GC) wants to know where the power is for the generator. The crew was busy the entire time doing bona fide electrical work, but now, in addition to re-wiring the basement, they also have to remove materials they installed on the seventh floor, potentially delaying other aspects of the project. The production is no further along, despite their efforts. The labor was busy, but as a result of miscommunication the outcome of their work is not considered CPIP because they have to reinstall all the work in the basement to get paid. In other words, first they installed the power on the seventh floor, and then they had to take it out and reinstall it in the basement. They do the work three times, but they get paid only once.

■ Production versus Productivity

The difference between production and productivity is simply what was done versus how well it was done. Production in construction measures the construction-put-in-place whereas productivity measures how well it was put in place. Ordinary accounting measurements of jobs in construction are measurements of production.

Suppose a contract calls for the installation of 500 fixtures. At the end of the project, production measures show that 500 fixtures were installed. However, consider the productivity impacts:

- Some of the fixtures arrived damaged from shipping. They had to be returned and replaced before they were installed.
- Some of the fixtures ordered never arrived. They were discontinued and replacements had to be found and approved. Incidentally, the replacements did not fit the same configuration and required a different wiring plan.
- Some of the fixtures installed were incorrect. They needed to be removed, returned, and replaced.
- Fixtures were installed in an incorrect location. They needed to be removed and repositioned.
- Some fixtures were installed by an apprentice; every step of the installation had to be laid out and double-checked.
- Some fixtures were delivered in August for installation in December. They were put into temporary storage in an unused area. The generator scheduled for that area arrived in September, so the fixtures were moved to a new temporary location.
- Some of the fixtures were stored (temporarily) in an offsite location that was not accessible the week the crew planned to begin installation.
- Other fixtures just "vanished." A few were never found and were reordered; others were found after replacements had been ordered, received, and installed, necessitating return of the extras or the original fixtures, which were well past the time frame for easy returns.

- The fixtures were intended to be hung by a single electrician. The crew found it easier to install them working in pairs, at only a slightly faster pace, thereby nearly doubling the labor requirements for installation.
- The fixtures were ordered to arrive preassembled. The preassembly only applied to the assembly of 2 of the 8 parts and 24 screws. Three of the parts actually came in a completely separate shipment.
- The electric screwdriver had a dead battery. Replacement tools came from the tool room a few days later. This meant that the crew couldn't finish the incomplete fixtures and had to wait another two or three days to get the right tools.

At the end of the project, 500 fixtures were installed. The production measures of 500 fixtures and $50,000 in revenue show that. The story these measures don't tell is that of productivity: what it took to install those 500 fixtures. The productivity tells how the fixtures were installed and what it actually took to accomplish the task. In this case, sidetracked effort dedicated to anything other than installation drove the productivity down and down and down. Although reordering material, for example, may be critical to the completion of the project, it doesn't move the project any closer to completion. Hanging fixtures at 4-ft intervals when they need to be at 5-ft intervals may have kept the electrician working, but, again, it does not bring the project closer to completion. The point here is that motion is not equal to work or CPIP if the motion is not adding any value from the customer's perspective. Just because the labor is on the job site and they do things does not mean that the job is making progress.

■ System Productivity

System productivity measures the productivity of the entire set of job site activities. You measure it by evaluating the hours used for installation or fabrication, which you are paid for, compared to the total hours used on the job site.

In other words, the productivity of the entire system is the contribution of the value-added hours divided by the total hours used to put the construction in place. Suppose, for example, that it takes an estimated 2 hours to install a fixture, but the electrician spends only 45 minutes of that time actually on installation and assembly. The electrician spends the remaining 1 hour and 15 minutes on various support activities: locating tools, unpackaging components, placing ladders, and so on. This noninstallation time is non-value-added, or unproductive. The system productivity is the ratio of 45 installation minutes to 120 total minutes, or 37.5 percent.

System productivity is the primary factor that affects the job's overall productivity. To increase the system productivity effectively, you must reduce the non-value-added work. Very often, electrical contractors and project managers ask themselves, "How do I get my workers to be more productive?" They are often surprised to find that labor does not think of solving job productivity issues in ways that contractors may think are the most logical. The real issue is typically not that labor does not know how to be productive, but rather that the difficulties lie with systems designed by contractors and project managers.

A correctly designed and applied system reduces the non-value-added work on the job site. However, it quickly becomes clear that nonproductive time and non-value-added activity have different meanings to the labor than they do to the contractor. For example, suppose the project manager orders all the material at once and has it drop-shipped to the job site (**FIGURE 2–1**). The labor has no choice but to receive and store the material. When the labor receives the material and stores it, and then later moves or returns it, he does not think that this work is nonproductive. He is giving the contractor a full day of work for a full day of pay. He does not know—or most of the time even care—whether the contractor is paid for material handling. He is doing what he has been asked to do, and

FIGURE 2–1 Labor is not productive when moving or storing material.

he deserves to be paid for it. He may not be installing, but he is working. What really is causing the labor to work on nonproductive tasks?

System productivity is the main factor driving the lack of Agility on the job site. The productivity loss shown in **FIGURE 2–2** is lost system productivity. To improve the system productivity, the system needs to be Agile. To really have the flexibility necessary to respond to changes on the job site, the entire system has to be designed from the labor's perspective. To make the system visible, data have to come from the technician—correctly, in a timely manner, and inexpensively. Later sections in this book look at the tools, processes, and concepts that make this happen, such as short-interval scheduling (SIS™), Job Productivity Assurance and Control (JPAC®), estimation analysis environment (EAE™), and processes including the process of procurement and the process of project management. Agile is at its best when you can bring together the elements that allow for visibility, flexibility, and responsiveness on the job site.

FIGURE 2–2 Material in this room will not be used here. Moving material is nonproductive.

■ Individual Productivity

Individual productivity is often identified and measured by the personal effort used toward getting things done. In the earlier example of preparing the seventh floor, the labor installed the conduit, pulled the wire, made the connections, and did everything that needed to be done. They used budgeted hours that had been allocated to that activity. Individually, they were productive, yet the task was ultimately unnecessary.

An individual's productivity is highly affected by the match between the required task and the electrician's skills, experience level, on-hand materials, tools, and schedule. Individual productivity depends on many factors including training, health, self-esteem, planning, even absenteeism—electricians can't work if they aren't there.

In contrast, system productivity is the productivity that is driven by all of the interactions between systems and individuals, both on the job site and within the company. System productivity is affected by company policies, procedures, and processes both independently and through their interactions. In the time to detect and time to react example presented earlier in Chapter 1, in addition to an invisible schedule and trade interference, the system productivity was affected by an ineffective ordering system. Research shows that 40 percent of the labor's time on the job site may be spent on material-handling issues such as this rather than on effective installation.

■ Measuring Production and Productivity

How do you measure productivity? Accounting software programs often claim to provide productivity calculations. In reality, these are production calculations, straight production measures of installation per unit of time (for example, 20 feet of wire per hour), which is not equal to job site productivity. These methods do not show the ongoing changes in the field labor productivity. They only focus on the average hours used to put construction in place.

System productivity cannot be measured based on an individual's output. You must measure productivity in terms of the actual work required for completion from the customer's perspective. You must measure the changes in productivity caused by job conditions to accurately react to obstacles that reduce the installation time and therefore worsen the productivity.

Consider this scenario: One thousand feet of conduit laid in a straight line is not the same as a thousand feet of conduit with 90° drops and multiple turns. If a crew installs 1250 feet of conduit in 2 days, it appears that 625 feet can be installed per day. In reality, one day the crew was able to install 1000 feet in 8 hours and the other day they were able to install 250 feet in 8 hours (**FIGURE 2–3**). The actual capability of the crew is lost because the two days of time include mobilization, meeting delivery trucks, waiting for an area to clear, looking for tools, and other noninstallation activities.

Projections made based on day 1 will be substantially different from those based on day 2 and from those based on an average. Unless you understand the underlying cause, these variations in job site predictability carry through and show up substantially as variations in the company's work in process

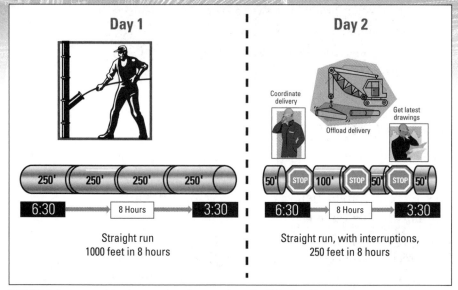

FIGURE 2–3 Average labor hour per foot does not show the difficulty of installation.

(WIP) projections, with a significant impact on billing and cash flow.

Using labor for any purpose other than installation or installation-related activities such as fabrication can turn a job from a potentially profitable, successful project into a money loser. It can even turn it into a "killer job" that single-handedly wipes away all profits made by every other project in the company. Without actual measures of productivity that recognize variation, cost accounting, and quantity measures, you are unable to provide accurate assessments of job progress, productivity, work in process, and profitability.

■ Managing the Productivity

Productivity is closely tied to profits. By using productivity-based measurements in the field as well as in the office, you can move from strictly after-the-fact recording on the job to capturing timely information that you can use to manage the job directly. During the estimation process, you evaluate a project to determine how it will go in, what it will cost based on that evaluation, and a reasonable markup. If the labor is able to improve upon the expected productivity so that the work is performed significantly better than planned, the difference contributes to increased profits. If the labor works less productively than planned, the difference is paid for by the contractor out of the expected profits of the project. **FIGURE 2–4** clearly indicates the relationship on these jobs between labor productivity on the job site and the final profitability as measured in accounting.

Consider another scenario: 100 fixtures to install, with an estimated labor cost of 2 hours to complete the installation for each fixture with a sample labor rate of $50 per hour and an estimated material cost of $100 each. After 16 hours, 8 fixtures have been installed. Material costs at this point are essentially fixed: you need 100 of the $100 fixtures, so material costs are $10,000. Labor costs are on target because 16 hours at the hourly rate is exactly where you expected to be. You have installed 8 fixtures in 16 hours, an average of 2 hours per fixture.

However, these are the production numbers. Labor productivity issues cannot be seen. Suppose the first 8 individual fixtures were installed as shown in **FIGURE 2–5**. The first four fixtures took 2 hours each; the 5th took only 1 hour; the 6th and 7th required 1.5 hours, and the 8th took 4 hours. The reasons for

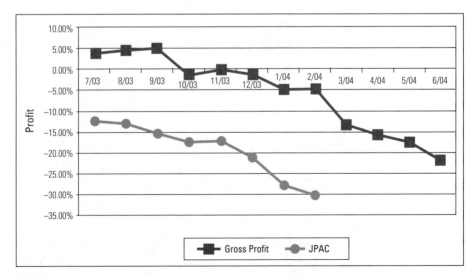

FIGURE 2–4 The trend in job productivity assurance and control (JPAC) is leading the gross profitability trend on this project.

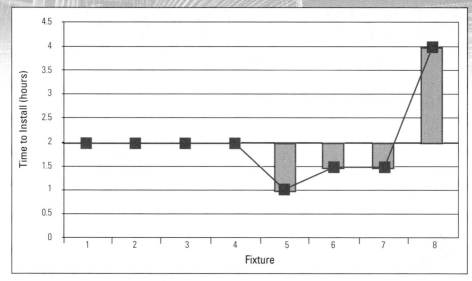

FIGURE 2–5 System impacts on productivity are masked if you monitor only average production.

this variation can be many and are discussed in a later section; however, the production numbers are unable to show this difference. A more experienced electrician may have installed the 5th fixture; the 6th and 7th fixtures may have been closer to the material storage site. The 8th may have been in an area with a 12-ft ceiling instead of an 8-ft ceiling, or may have been missing a component, or may have included time to remove all the packaging from the 8 fixtures. Without knowing there is such a difference, you are at risk, and without knowing why, you can do little to improve the situation.

Because completion of the project task requires the installation of all 100 fixtures, the productivity is critical to the final profitability of the project. Considering only this task, if the productivity can be maintained at what is so far the average pace, the labor costs will be as expected: 100 fixtures at 2 hours each at $50 per hour would meet the originally estimated labor cost of $10,000. If the productivity can be increased so that it can be maintained at the 1-hour pace as for fixture 5, the remaining 92 fixtures plus the 16 hours used for the first 8 would require only $5400 for labor. The difference goes straight to the contractor in the form of profits. However, if the remaining fixtures all take the 4 hours as needed for fixture 8, the remaining 92 fixtures would require an additional 368 hours plus the first 16 hours. These 384 hours would cost a total of $19,200; this is $9200 more than estimated and almost double the original labor cost estimate of $10,000. The additional $9200 comes straight out of the project's profits.

Standard accounting measures of job progress often substitute the percent usage of estimated costs or percentage used of estimated hours in place of the physically observed percentage complete. Measuring the job cost measures only production, not productivity. For an effective measure of Agility, you must track labor productivity from the labor's perspective.

By measuring labor productivity using accounting methods, you can move hours from one cost code (the allocated cost of each estimated activity) to another, which often masks the productivity changes. The contractor will pay for eight hours of work; however, he will never know which cost codes cost him how much. Productivity delays and their resulting impacts may not be recognized until the end of the project when they are both most visible and most costly (**FIGURE 2–6**).

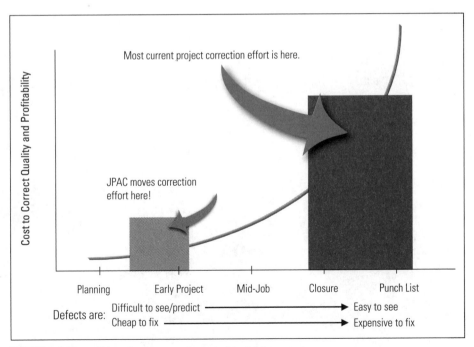

FIGURE 2–6 Recognition of problems at the end of the job is expensive.

An Agile Construction company must have a culture focused not only on labor productivity, but on doing the right things at the right time. An Agile company cannot afford wasted labor; eliminating waste in the system frees resources so that you can focus them on the effective completion of the project.

Making It Visible

The old saying is as true today as when it was first said: "What gets measured gets done." It is also true that only what is visible gets measured. The logical consequence is that to measure and manage construction activities, you must make the activities visible. Once you make the activities visible through the use of the Agile tools, you can categorize them to separate the productive activities from the nonproductive ones.

All the activities in any organization can be divided into three categories:

- Productive, also called value-add
- Nonproductive (non-value-add) but necessary (due to regulations or other requirements)
- Nonproductive (non-value-add) and not necessary

The nonproductive activities do not directly contribute to the final product and ultimately result in wasted effort regardless of necessity driven by the system. For example, having material available on the top floor is a necessity for installation; however, waiting for the lift to bring the material is not a requirement because coordination or planning could have avoided that scenario.

Activities that an electrician performs, from manning the project until project completion, include the following:

- Plan for work areas (manpower, material, tools needed)
- Lay out work area
- Review work plan with the crew
- Install
- Preassemble or prefabricate

- Repair temporary power for other contractors
- Detail (red-lines, as-builts)
- Handle material (looking for, ordering, following up, moving, receiving, preparing returns)
- Report on installation and crew
- Inspect

The system requires some nonproductive activity. For example, waiting for an inspection from the general contractor (GC) may be critical, yet does little to help the project proceed physically. Better planning could minimize wasted or misused time, effort, material, and money.

Effort expended on any of the following unnecessary activities adds bulk to the system and reduces agility:

- *Overproduction.* Having more capacity than the job requires. For example, increasing manpower when the job is peaking or is falling behind schedule for reasons other than manpower.
- *Transportation.* Movement of material or labor that does not add value. For example, electricians walking up a flight of stairs (or two) every time something is needed from the gang box.
- *Waiting.* Idle time created when material, information, or people are not ready; labor is waiting for instructions, fabrication machines are idling, or crews are waiting on material.
- *Motion.* Activities that do not add value such as storing material at a distance from the point of installation, for example, in an offsite facility.
- *Overprocessing/overengineering.* Efforts that create no value from the customer's viewpoint, such as writing multiple purchase orders, handling material multiple times, or adding unnecessary packaging material.
- *Inventory.* Ordering, handling, and storing material before it is ready for installation.
- *Defects/rejects/rework.* Errors, omissions, mistakes, and rework.

See **TABLE 3–1**.

TABLE 3-1 **Seven Types of Waste in a System**	
Overproduction	Generating more than the customer needs right now
Transportation	Movement of product or supplies that does not add value
Waiting	Idle time created when material, information, people, or equipment is not ready
Motion	Movement of people that does not add value
Overprocessing	Processing efforts that create no value from the customer's viewpoint
Inventory	More information, project, or material on hand than the customer needs right now
Defects/Rejects/ Rework	Work that contains errors, rework, or mistakes, or that lacks something necessary

Each of these activities impairs productivity on the job site and always results in increased waste and reduced output per resources used.

A second factor, variation, adds to the waste by further affecting job productivity. You can see variation, or inconsistencies, in the following areas:

- Job to job
- Foreman to foreman
- Project manager to project manager
- Electrician to electrician
- Estimate to job
- Estimate to estimate
- Vendor to vendor
- GC to GC

You can make both waste and variation visible by using the tools available in Agile Construction™. Waste is a well-understood activity in construction. Variation, on the other hand, needs a bit more explanation.

What Is Variation?

It is a recognized fact in construction that every job is different. Why does one day go exactly right when everything that could go wrong does go wrong the very next day? The answer to that lies in variation. Variation is a deviation from the expected outcome. Variation in any form causes inconsistencies and prevents consistent, repeatable production. Two otherwise identical jobs can result in vastly different profits because of the market, the location, the materials, the schedule, the crew, the owner, the weather, and a myriad of other reasons. A rear-view accounting measure of the cost and quantities does not even begin to address why one job may lose 5 percent while the other makes 30 percent.

How to See the Variation

You can feel variation on the job site in the daily ups and downs. However, to understand the impact of variation on the job and labor productivity, you have to make it visible.

One method of making variation visible is by using run charts to record events in time sequence so that you can monitor trends. For example, you can track a job that is currently predicting the labor to be 18 percent more productive than expected; at first, translating that into profits may sound great until you realize that the job had been predicting 25 percent or 30 percent additional labor productivity.

FIGURE 3–1 shows two jobs from their Job Productivity Assurance and Control (JPAC®) charts (see Part II for details). One

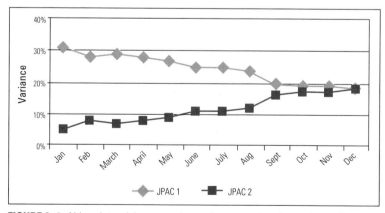

FIGURE 3–1 Although two jobs may end up at the same point, they took two different paths to get there.

is trending downward from 30 percent productivity; the second one is trending upward from 2 percent to 18 percent. Job 2 has been gaining momentum from the start, lessons learned are incorporated into ongoing work, planning is used, advantages are capitalized upon, and the productivity has been steadily increasing as the job progresses. Job 1, however, also shows a productivity measurement of 18 percent more productive than planned, but this job has been losing ground since the beginning. It started in January with a great showing, almost 30 percent more productive than planned. Since then, this job has encountered problems and issues typical to every job site, such as other trades in the way, schedule changes, incomplete material deliveries, lack of access, weather, and absenteeism.

Although both jobs currently show the labor progressing 18 percent more productively than planned, the trend of the productivity, that is, how it got to 18 percent, is more important than the 18 percent itself. If the jobs continue much longer, job 1 could be in considerable trouble, whereas job 2 has the potential to do very well. The trend shows what the static measurement does not. On job 1, 18 percent is a liability—the early productivity gains on the job were lost. On job 2, 18 percent is an immense improvement. It is important to notice that at this stage the accounting numbers, however, show exactly the same result.

As demonstrated, without complete information, the current productivity or profit numbers may look good for both jobs, but the reality is somewhat different. Increased productivity is directly correlated to increased profitability. With correct and timely intervention enabled by Agile processes, you could recognize the situations causing a decline in productivity and address them so that the productivity rate can be maintained. The only way to stop the downward trend on job 1 is to know what is occurring as it occurs. By using trend monitoring and other aspects of statistical process control (SPC), you could recognize the warning signals and respond to them immediately.

Control Signals

Every process, just like every product, has certain outputs that define its behavior. For example, when a hand drill gets hot or starts to smell, the electrician knows that the drill may be overworked or require repair. Although a process may not start to smell, indicators of the process can alert you to problems that are developing or that already exist. One way you can see the indicators of change in a process is to observe changes in numerical indicators, such as labor hours or cost codes or productivity. By creating a run chart from the process-related numbers, you can see whether something is wrong with the process performance and can even predict what might happen next.

Several control signals indicate the presence of special causes or problems with the process (**FIGURE 3–2A–E**). In sta-

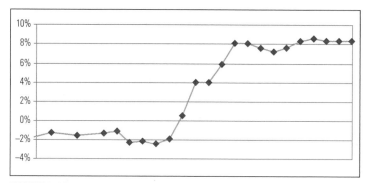

FIGURE 3–2A Process control signals: Trend: 5–6 points in a row (up or down).

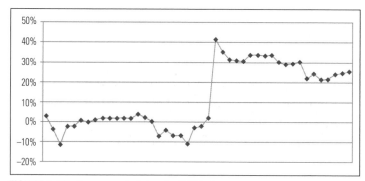

FIGURE 3–2B Process control signals: Shift in the mean.

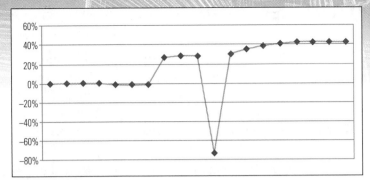

FIGURE 3–2C Process control signals: Extreme point.

FIGURE 3–2D Process control signals: Saw teeth.

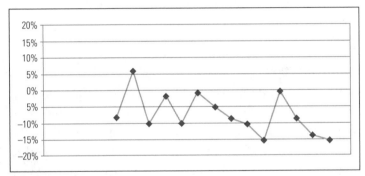

FIGURE 3–2E Process control signals: No reporting.

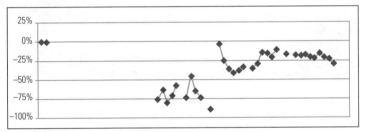

tistics, the random or accidental occurrence of any of these problems in a trend is reason enough to consider the existence of an outside influence, just as the heat of the drill suggests a problem. For example, the drill may overheat because the electrician has overworked it or because it is getting old, but in either case, something special is going on. Similarly, once you have identified in a process a control signal that suggests a special cause, you must use other methods to identify the underlying reason for the signal.

Control signals have unique characteristics that you can clearly spot in a trend. These signals are not likely to appear by accident. Here are some of the signals:

1. *Trends:* Five or six consecutive points moving in the same direction
2. *Shifts in the mean:* Nine points in a row on one side of the mean
3. *Outlier point:* One point more than three standard deviations from the mean
4. *Saw teeth:* Fourteen ups and downs in a row
5. *Missing data:* No data available

Trends: Several Consecutive Points Moving in the Same Direction

A run chart that shows a trend upward or downward that continues for more than five or six points is typically signaling an anomaly or special cause. A trend of five or six points in the same direction is often considered a strong enough signal to which you should react because this should happen by chance less than 3 percent of the time (**FIGURE 3–3**).

Shifts in the Mean: Nine Points in a Row on One Side of the Mean

A shift in the mean (the average) is another indication of a special cause. This typically occurs when at least nine points

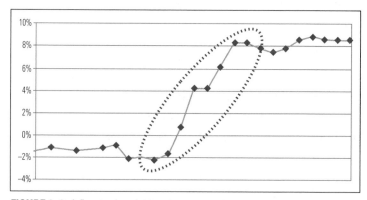

FIGURE 3–3 A five- to six-point trend.

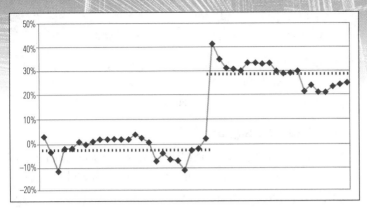

FIGURE 3–4 Shift in the mean.

in a row fall on one side of the mean and the rest of the points fall on the other side of the mean (**FIGURE 3–4**).

One Point More Than Three Standard Deviations from the Mean

In a normal distribution, 68 percent of the data fall within one standard deviation (1σ) and another 27 percent of the data fall between 1 and 2 sigma. Variation in this range and this pattern is expected. Deviations from this pattern trigger special cause control signals (**FIGURE 3–5**).

Saw Teeth: 14 Ups and Downs in a Row

Points on a run chart that alternate vigorously indicate lack of control of the process. When the data points go up, and then

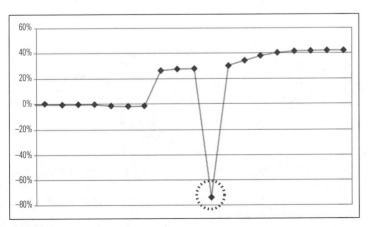

FIGURE 3–5 One point out of the ordinary.

down, and then up, and then down and this occurs 14 times in a row, a special cause is likely indicated (**FIGURE 3–6**).

Missing Data

Missing data is a clear indication of lack of process control and requires immediate attention (**FIGURE 3–7**).

How to Read the Signals

Control signals are strong enough signals that they occur naturally less than 4 times out of every 1000 opportunities. In practice, it is often reasonable to respond to even weaker signals in the trend while realizing that there is a good possibility that the signal could have occurred by chance rather than by

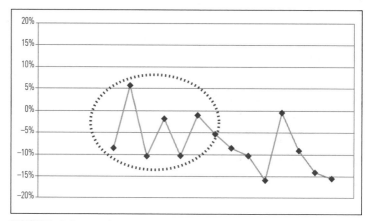

FIGURE 3–6 Saw-tooth pattern.

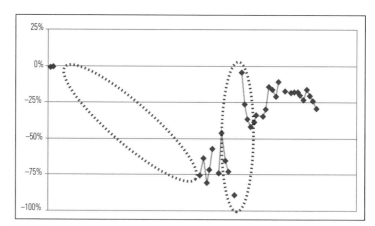

FIGURE 3–7 Missing data or no reporting.

cause. For example, a trend of five consecutive points all moving downward can happen by chance less than 3 percent of the time. This is enough of a trend to suggest that there is likely an identifiable cause, but you should also recognize the fact that occasionally it can happen as a result of the expected common cause variation driven by the system itself.

Other signals also can indicate a need for investigation. Unreported data may mean the data suggest bad news; for example, performance on the job was not what it should have been and the reporting was not completed to cover up for the underperformance. If the project manager believes he can make up the difference the next week, he may delay reporting. A repeating cycle may suggest a regular outside influence; for example, job site deliveries may regularly take 20 to 25 minutes, but every Friday they take 35 to 40 minutes. Something is likely to be happening on Fridays, even though the deviation may not trigger or be within control limits. Upon further investigation, you may find a different driver delivers on Fridays, or the foreman conducts a meeting at the regular delivery time and the extra time is spent waiting or searching for him, or two deliveries usually arrive at the same time on Fridays, or the delivery occurs at 10 on Fridays but at 7:30 on other days, or even just that donuts are on the delivery truck on Fridays.

FIGURE 3–8 shows a system-level example of the two types of variation: special cause variation and common cause variation. Common cause variation is caused by internal processes at the company level and is evident in the many small ups and downs. Special cause variation appears when the control signals show an occurrence that is unexpected or outside the normal operations.

Special cause variation has a more pronounced immediate effect on the trend than common cause variation does. You can usually attribute the reason for the variation to a distinct event. In this case, asking "What happened?" is extremely productive. This question can lead you to identify the root cause and provide a focus point for improving the situation and eliminating the cause. On the other hand, asking "what happened?" to

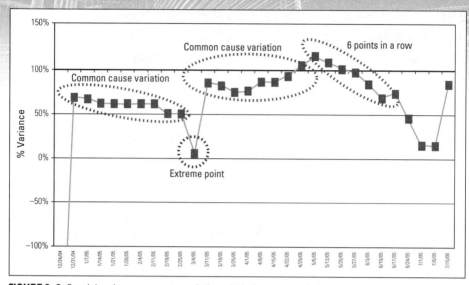

FIGURE 3–8 Special and common cause variation within the same project.

find the cause of every little variation is a low-yield and costly strategy.

There are two types of mistakes that electrical contractors make when dealing with variation:

Mistake 1: Mistreating common cause variation as special cause variation

Mistake 2: Mistreating special cause variation as common cause variation

An example of mistake 1 is overadjustment—implementing rigid approval and sign-off procedures, requiring multiple copies of POs, controlling minutely detailed procedures, or creating just-in-case inventory—to buffer every up and down. To reduce the variation and improve the predictability, you need to improve the process. On the other hand, never trying to find a special cause and just assuming "that's the way it goes" is an example of mistake 2. You need to make a specific appropriate response to a one-time occurrence.

Both mistakes are costly, and although it is impossible to totally eliminate both mistakes all the time, your goal should be to minimize the net economic loss from these mistakes. By appropriately responding to the control signals, you can manage both mistakes effectively.

If you cannot see either of these mistakes, the costs can be high and oftentimes are unrecoverable. Cost-based measurement after construction progress costs productivity and hides the causes under averages. Moving events from one cost code to another can further mask the special causes so that you address them as though they are common causes on the job or ongoing effects of the system. On the other hand, quantity measurements may show a single cost code's common cause variation as a special cause, triggering management to react to the variation incorrectly and resulting in tampering with the common cause variation.

JPAC (see Chapter 8) measures productivity based on actual construction-put-in-place (CPIP). JPAC identifies the underlying cause of variation as a systematic issue or a special cause so that you can respond correctly and manage the job more effectively.

Short Interval Scheduling (SIS™; also discussed in Chapter 8) measures the results of the day-to-day items that affect the job, identifying root causes of common cause variation. You can use SIS to help identify the immediate reasons for a sudden swing in productivity; however, you can also use it to identify the systematic issues that need to be managed to maintain better control and predictability on the job. Day-to-day repetitive interruptions disrupt progress and affect productivity. By documenting obstacles that affect the completion of the first day of the foreman's three-day look-ahead, you can see the systemic and systematic interruptions. For example, if the plumber is in your way, you cannot complete Schedule A for today. When you know that this kind of trade interference occurs every day on the job site, you can make the system-level changes that will reduce the common cause variation.

When both SIS and JPAC show reduced variation and improved predictability, you can then apply focused effort to improve the measurements. This has the additional benefit of creating a more predictable job site, cash flow, and labor management with the resulting net effect of increased profitability on the job and reduced costs.

Variation in Construction

Everyone in construction feels and knows that variation exists. It would be much more surprising and unexpected if things were constant and predictable. Variation, even in small aspects of an electrical contractor's work, affects the profitability of the entire operation. Although the labor may not be the direct source of the variation, any kind of variation throughout your company's operation is reflected in labor productivity, with a substantial impact on both system productivity and overall profitability. Making predictions in the face of unpredictable variation is difficult. When the decisions an EC makes do not occur as expected, more often than not the business will lose.

Each day electrical contractors decide (predict) whether to bid work, hire labor, schedule material shipments, and much more. Every day contractors must think: "If I take this action, then I will get this (desired) result" (**FIGURE 3–9**). For example: "If I bid the job at this amount, I will win the job and make a profit," or, "If I put five men on this job today, I will be able to complete the branch wiring," or, "If I order material to be delivered on that date, I will be ready to use it then and I will not have workers waiting for it to arrive." Each action the contractor takes is based on confidence in the outcome of those decisions and predictions. The success or failure of the business hinges on the quality of the decisions and on the effectiveness of the predictions made. The tools and processes of Agile Construc-

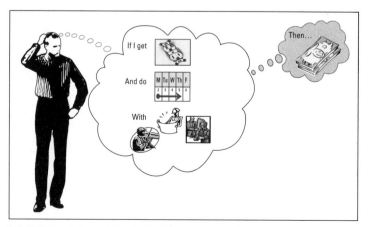

FIGURE 3–9 Daily decisions that affect the project outcome.

tion make the system visible, allowing deeper understanding of the causes of unpredictability and providing the information to allow the next decision to be the correct one.

Other industries have learned that variation affects all aspects of operation; from office work to field support, from labor management to project management, from material management to supplier relationships, and from foreman to foreman. By managing variation in many aspects of their work, companies in other industries have been able to stay competitive against low-cost producers.

Mismanagement of variation allows uncertainty to determine profits and often reduces them. In everyday construction, variation shows in the following formats:

- Job to job
- Estimate to job
- Estimate to estimate

All the other types of variations mentioned earlier such as project manager to project manager or foreman to foreman are derivatives of these three variation types.

Job-to-Job Variation

Very often contractors run similar or the same exact jobs over a period of time and get completely different results each time. In electrical contracting, you can see the impact of variation on time, cost, and quality in the following examples:

- Variations in timing (including schedule changes) can cause, at a minimum, wasted labor hours caused by wait time and, in the extreme, damage liquidation charges.
- Variations in cost caused by adding material costs or handling costs and rework that is not anticipated in the estimate can reduce profits.
- Variations in quality can occur as a result of hampering the installation, function, or reliability, or by not satisfying the end customer.

The greater the variation, the more severe the impact of uncertainty on the contractor's profitability. You can see the impact of variation in the ultimate unpredictability of your profits. **FIGURE 3–10** shows a representative electrical contractor's percentage of profitability by job throughout a year. Although the average shows what may be an acceptable 14.7 percent gross profit overall on projects, individual projects vary widely, recognizing anywhere from a 40 percent profit to a 16 percent loss. In this example, the standard deviation is 13.4 percent, indicating that on average the next job might earn as high as 28.1 percent or as low as 1.3 percent gross profit.

This spread is far too wide to allow reliable predictions of profits. For a $100,000 job, for example, this is a potential difference between earning a profit of $28,100 or $1300. If the job is larger, the difference multiplies as well. A typical $1,000,000 job would have an expected profit of either $280,000 or $13,000, a $267,000 difference; for a $10,000,000 job, the difference becomes $2,670,000. In some cases, this potential difference in profitability can be more than the entire net profit of the company the previous year—and exactly what sets up the potential for killer jobs. It is virtually impossible to determine, even approximately, what the profitability of the next project will be. This lack of predictability from job to job makes it challenging for an electrical contractor to manage cash flow, meet financial obligations, and accurately bid for new work.

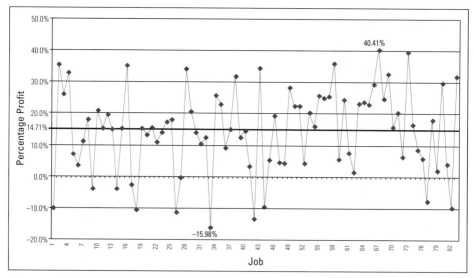

FIGURE 3–10 Typical EC job-to-job profitability.

Estimate-to-Job Variation

Very often you hear that estimation in construction is an art and not a science that can be taught through the regular channels of construction education. This perception is borne out by the fact that estimators go through many years of trial and error to gain enough experience to estimate jobs close to the actual performance of the labor. A very good estimator for one contractor can become a bad estimator for another if he has not had a chance to correct for errors caused by the difference in labor performance between the two companies. A good estimate can go bad with poor field management, and a productive labor force can make even a bad estimate profitable.

The vigorous and unpredictable oscillation in between the expected outcome and the actual outcome of construction jobs has a number of sources:

1. *Inaccurate field reporting of labor hours.* The historical approach to labor hour reporting from the field, whether by cost codes or by the total hours used, has evolved based on the estimator's need for an accurate measure of the labor used. Because it is not needed for the field, the reporting of the labor hours does not help the labor to do a better job or monitor their productivity performance. The electricians report their hours to get paid. They have no advantage or disadvantage for allocating and reporting correctly to individual cost codes. If there are too many cost codes, it becomes virtually impossible for them to allocate a day's work correctly. Hours are dumped wherever there are hours left in the budget. And, at the end of the day, the electricians get paid regardless of whether they allocated the hours correctly or not.

2. *The labor reports their hours to match the estimate (or to do the estimator a favor).* "Tell me how you will measure me; I'll tell you how I'll respond." Often the field is given a construction budget and is expected to match it, despite the fact that the estimator may have arrived at the estimate in a very different way than how the work will actually proceed. Jobs are rarely installed in the same way they are estimated. Most

often, estimation is done with good intentions, trying to quantify a complicated situation.

For example, the estimator may estimate the job based on the number of assemblies, in which case a motor assembly may become a cost code for the purpose of estimation. However, the pipe, wire, termination, commissioning, and other activities associated with the motor assembly may be installed in a different sequence for every assembly, making it virtually impossible for the field labor to narrow down their labor tracking to give accurate total assembly hours. In addition, parts of several assemblies may be worked on at the same time, making it even more difficult to distinguish the labor required for a single assembly and rendering the assembly inefficient as a tracking cost code. Reliance on the field labor report for estimation accuracy in this situation is like measuring the number of door knobs to estimate the hours needed for bus-duct. If the contractor is using cost codes to collect labor hour data, he must be sure that the cost codes and the way the data are requested for collection match the way the jobs are installed.

3. *The estimate itself.* Even though the actual estimation is seldom the cause of variation in the job's outcome, electricians will tell you more often than not that the estimate is off. What they typically mean is that the hours allocated to each activity or cost code in the estimate are not in line with what they need to finish the job. They aren't working the job in the same way that it was estimated. However, in many legitimate examples the actual takeoff and accounting accuracy of the estimate are wrong and cause unpredictable outcomes in the job. For example, when estimators miscount, misallocate, and completely miss a system such as fire alarm. No matter how diligent the electrician does his job, he will still lose money on the job.

4. *Manpower.* The quality, training, and background of the labor can have a huge impact on the outcome of the job and on the difference between the estimated and the actual outcome of the project. For example, in tight economic times, a company may reduce to its "core" electricians,

improving productivity with a well-trained, cohesive group that is familiar with the company's work style, policies, and processes. In good economic times, when a lot of work is available, the effective labor shortage may cause the company to use different labor on the job than was planned at the time of the estimate. New electricians are brought into the company, new foremen are created as the jobs come on faster than the system can handle. New work requiring different training and experience can come in either situation—in good economic times or in a shrinking economy—in either case, the workforce is fluctuating with a noticeable effect on project outcomes.

Another result of either tight or booming markets is that the available work may change. For example, if most jobs available are commercial jobs and the company has historically performed industrial work, the company has more electricians trained in industrial installation than in commercial, so picking up additional commercial work requires different skills, experience, and processes. Using a workforce with industrial background on a commercial job or vice versa can cause major variation in the outcome.

5. *Material management.* Management of the material, manpower, and money distinguishes one job from the next. Which is more important? The money recovered from returned materials or the labor's time spent preparing and returning the material, not to mention the time lost in acquiring material that was not used on the job site in the first place? The project manager must make the correct decision based on the data—is lost labor worth more than the return value of the material? Often this is the case. However, when the material cost is visible, and the labor cost is hidden, it is easy to focus the manager's attention on the wrong things.

   Jobs do change, and material needs usually change with them. A job with significant change orders is penalized even more because a large number of labor hours are wasted dealing with returns. MCA Inc.'s data show that the cost recovery from returned material on average for the entire year is less than 1 percent of the annual sales, whereas the labor cost to deal with the returns could be as high as 5 percent of annual sales. A 4 percent increase in net profit could be recognized simply by writing off the material.

6. *Job site conditions.* Estimates are often made without the luxury of knowing the job site conditions. Every variation in the conditions affects the labor, the timing, the job site needs, and so on. Every change, alteration, or anomaly in the conditions that was unknown or unknowable during the estimation has a distinct impact on the job's outcome.

For example, a job could be estimated for a start in the summer; however, a 6-month delay can easily force the project to start in the winter instead. The impact of the weather can be either positive or negative on the job's outcome. The estimator did not figure into the estimate the delay caused by shoveling out from a March snowstorm because the job was originally scheduled to be completed in September. Or the estimator included delays for ground work scheduled for March, but the area experiences an unusually mild spring.

Access to the job site and amount of space available for tools, equipment, rentals, and material may be different and/or more limited than what was promised or assumed during the estimation phase. What looks good on paper may not be so good in three dimensions. For example, although the drawings show the exterior of the building, they do not note the fact that the building next door is a mere 3 feet away. If the crew planned to use the alley as a lay-down site, they must change their plans. Also, parking in a downtown location may be inaccessible, adding 30 to 40 minutes of lost time to every trip and excessive additional cost for nearby locations.

7. *General contractor (GC) or contract manager (CM).* Every electrical contractor knows that the GC or CM affects the outcome of the job. This is such an important factor that you should deal with it at the onset of the job estimate. The variation comes through the GC's selection and coordination of the following items:

- Other subcontractors
- Project management
- Self-performing tasks
- Safety and drug policies
- Schedule management
- Communications means
- Invoicing schedule
- Payment frequency
- Meetings
- Response to requests for quotes (RFQs) and requests for information (RFIs)
- Management of cut sheets
- Many other items

All of these drive the electrical contractor's performance on the job, as well as the performance of the other subs. Every one of these items must be integrated to make the system function in a way that brings together the installation of the entire project.

Estimate-to-Estimate Variation

Two companies bid the same job: One bids $680,000, and the other bids $750,000. If the job costs $600,000 to build, the first bid makes 11.7 percent, the other earns 20 percent. No one is surprised; one company has a competitive advantage over the other. This is a typical scenario that distinguishes contractors and their market penetration: With the same takeoff, two different estimators can arrive at two different numbers.

Comparable jobs can have very different outcomes. **FIGURE 3–11** shows estimation analysis of an electrical contractor. Bidding comparable jobs in various locations has resulted in different outcomes because of factors that the estimator could not have known at the time of bid. For example, a bid is in his local area may require an add-factor to the labor hours for pipe or wire and a subtract-factor for fixtures. If the same estimator uses comparable factoring tactics to win jobs in areas other than his local area, the estimates will be off because he developed the estimating factors based on the dominating conditions in

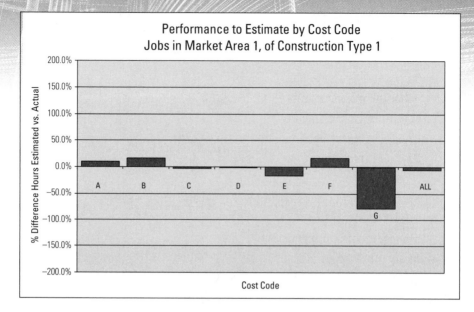

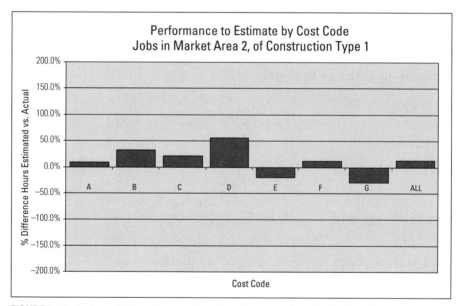

FIGURE 3–11 Analysis of job performance to estimate by geography and type of work.

his local area, which may not exist in other areas. The performance of the field and the variation of the job environment
can cause estimates to vary even if they are estimates for the
comparable jobs.

Making Money

Financial Models

Is it more important to save 1 percent of labor cost or 1 percent of overhead cost? The answer depends on the financial model your company uses. If your company is variable and labor-cost-heavy, 1 percent labor savings will be more beneficial. If your company is fixed-cost-heavy, reduction of overhead can help improve profits.

You can recognize profits only after you cover the fixed and variable costs of operations. The break-even point is the point at which your company first starts making money, where revenues first exceed costs. Fixed costs include general and administrative costs, insurance, property, and other fixed expenses, such as salaried office personnel and project managers or estimators. Fixed costs are the costs you must pay to operate the business, and they typically remain constant throughout the year. Variable costs are the costs associated with completing a project that are affected by the size of the project, for example, direct labor and incentives. Variable costs increase as sales increase because of the larger scope of the projects.

The generic profitability model shown in **FIGURE 4–1** illustrates the relationship between net profit, variable costs, and fixed costs. To recognize a profit, earned revenues must exceed both variable costs and fixed costs. The break-even point (BEP) is the point at which both variable and fixed costs are covered. Optimal performance occurs when both variable and fixed costs are minimized through error reduction, process improvement, and customer awareness.

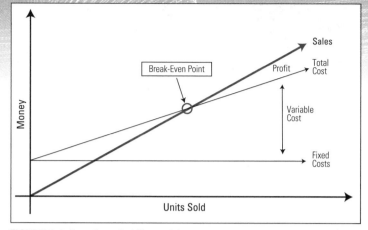

FIGURE 4–1 Generic profitability model.

■ Variable Cost Financial Model

Electrical contractors allocate the majority of their costs to individual projects. The cost of materials and the cost of labor
vary based on the requirements of the job. Many electrical
contractors recover their fixed operating costs by allocating a
portion of the amount incurred to each job (**FIGURE 4–2**). This
model recognizes nearly all costs as variable costs, that is, as
costs that increase relative to scope increases in the project.
Indirect labor, including administrative personnel, purchasing,
and managerial resources, often falls under fixed costs.

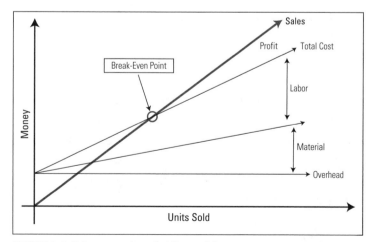

FIGURE 4–2 Subcontractor's profitability model.

In the variable cost financial model, the majority of overall expenses that the electrical contractor incurs over the life of a job are variable costs. By targeting and improving the variable costs, you can decrease the cost of each unit, or each dollar, of installation. This reduces the slope of the variable cost line, which lowers the overall cost. This is shown in **FIGURE 4–3** as the variable cost (VC) moves to the new variable cost level (VC-1). The fixed costs remain constant; the total cost, the sum of all fixed plus variable costs, is still reduced. This reduction again lowers the break-even point, which is illustrated by BEP moving leftward to BEP-1, and contributes directly to an increase in profit margin.

■ Fixed Cost Financial Model

In contrast to the variable cost model, general contractors, construction managers, and much of the construction supply chain allocate most of their costs to fixed costs (**FIGURE 4–4**).

In the fixed cost model, the fixed operational costs establish the base line of the total cost. For every dollar of fixed cost reduction, the variable cost base line drops by one dollar. The

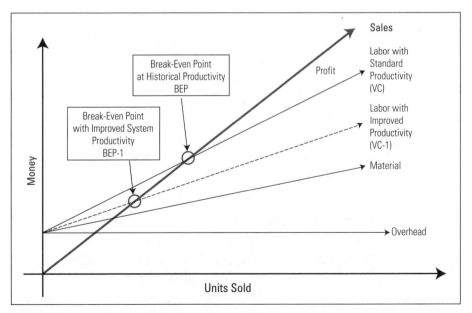

FIGURE 4–3 Impact of variable cost reduction on profitability.

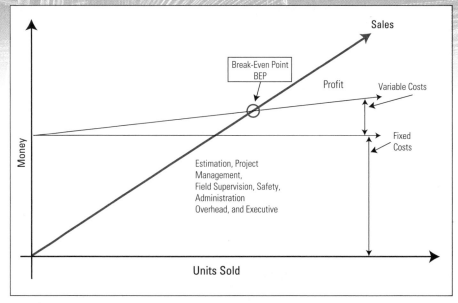

FIGURE 4–4 Fixed cost–driven profitability model.

fixed cost operator realizes a bigger impact on total cost reduction by targeting and reducing the fixed costs. **FIGURE 4–5** shows the effect of reducing the fixed costs (FC) to a new level (FC-1). This reduction creates a new base line to which any remaining variable costs are added. Even if variable costs remain at the same level as before, the total cost (the sum of fixed plus variable costs) is reduced by the savings amount, shown in Figure 4–5 by VC with FC to VC with FC-1. This reduction lowers the break-even point, which is illustrated by BEP moving leftward to BEP-1. This occurs earlier in the cycle, either at an earlier point in time or with fewer units sold, and contributes directly to an increase in the profit margin.

The differences between the two financial models drive the company's operations. As electrical contractors coordinate the job progress with project owners, GCs, and distributors, their main focus is to reduce the labor cost, or in other words to reduce their variable costs. Every additional hour in job labor drives your costs upward. In contrast, you might indiscriminately allocate to a job the fixed costs of project management, truck drivers, salespeople, time and materials (T&M), workers, and others. When the fixed cost resources are already part of the job cost, what they do for

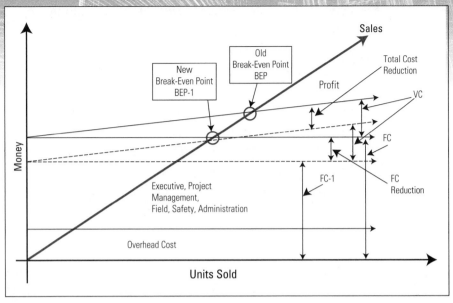

FIGURE 4–5 Impact of fixed cost reduction on profitability.

the job and its productivity is easily hidden. By effectively applying fixed cost workers' time, you can help the project to proceed
more productively by allowing the labor to move closer to the
ideal model of purely productive installation.

Where Does the Money Come From?

Contractors have three profit sources:

- Negotiated profits
- Profits in the operation from productivity
- Profits through reduced cost of cash flow

Negotiated profits are tracked using standard accounting
practices. Typically, the other two profit sources are untracked
and often unknown. The result is lump-sum cost allocation
to customers, resulting in unknown profitability of any given
project or customer.

Negotiated Profits

The historical margins earned through electrical contracting
have been dwindling. According to various national surveys,
the negotiated gross margins across the nation are currently

between 12 and 14 percent. The high margins found in the 1950s through the 1970s are no longer easily available.

The drop in margins comes largely from the shift of the construction market from high-profit industrial electrical work to lower-margin commercial and residential work. The onset of a service economy has shifted the nation's GDP from industrial sectors to service sectors and opened the doors for lower skilled electrical contractors. The proliferation in numbers of contractors across the commercial and residential segment has diluted the margins across the industry.

Naturally, the type of contract has a major impact on the estimated margins. Design-build, hard-bid, guaranteed-max-pricing, cost-plus, time and material, or any combination of the types of contracts used has its own characteristics when it comes to negotiated margins. However, overall, there is only so much that the contractor can ask for and the market will pay.

Increased Productivity

The primary means of increasing margins is through the labor. Small increases in productivity, with a culture focused on agility through continuous improvement and increased responsiveness, have substantial effects on the overall cost of the project.

To quantify this cost, here is a simple example. Assume that a particular job site is running with 10 electricians. Additionally, assume that most, but not all, of the deliveries are received as expected and as ordered, and that the loaded cost for labor is $40 per hour. As inconsistencies and last-minute changes drive the labor to work in different areas, or on different tasks than those planned, the interruption and realignment of workers result in a loss of productive effort.

Consider the effect of a loss of productive labor of even 12 minutes per day, or the equivalent loss of only 1 hour per week per worker: One hour per week per worker for the 10-person crew at $40 per hour equates to 1 hr/worker × $40/hr × 10 workers × 50 weeks/year = $20,000 per year in lost productivity on this one project.

You can expand this same example to measure the entire company. If the company employs 200 electricians at $40 per hour, then the resulting cost of lost productivity for every hour per week is $400,000 per year, or about 1.5 percent in additional net profit on a $25 million to $30 million company.

Every little reduction in nonproductive activity on the job site serves to lower the slope of the variable cost line, increasing profits by that much more (**FIGURE 4–6**).

Observations and measurements of the activities on the job site show an average of 40 percent of the labor's time is spent on the nonproductive activity that is not required for the installation. More than three hours a day typically goes to support activities: mobilizing, demobilizing, requesting material, waiting for material (or information), and receiving and preparing material for the actual installation.

For the company mentioned earlier, at the $40 hourly rate and 200 electricians, these three hours translate to $4,800,000 ($40 × 3 × 200 = $24,000/day, and $24,000 × 200 days/year = $4,800,000/year) of expense that is allocated to the job and therefore to the customer. Any reduction of this expense makes the company more competitive.

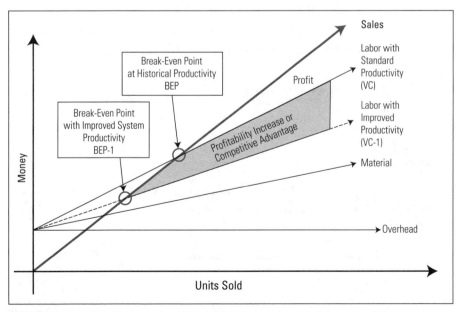

FIGURE 4–6 Gain in profits comes from the smallest change in improved labor productivity.

Reduced Cost of Cash Flow

Managing cash flow on construction projects is often more critical than attaining high profit margins when it comes to maintaining a healthy business. Contractors have come to expect large initial cash investments in their projects to get them started. The failure to monitor and manage cash flow can extend the duration of borrowing to the point that both the project and contractor can be jeopardized. Visibility allows better management and increases your opportunities to respond to the needs of the projects and the company—the cornerstone of Agility.

FIGURE 4–7 shows the cycle and logic of cash flow. Cash goes up when the cash payments are received, credit purchases are made, or sales are in cash. Cash goes down when cash payments are made, credit sales are approved, and cash purchases are made.

Underbilling in contracting happens when the job has been installed, the revenue has been recognized, but the customer has not yet been billed. Underbilling and accounts receivable are major sources of profit drain for contractors. The national average for underbilling for electrical contractors is approximately 10 percent of their annual sales revenue. A $10 million contractor can have $1 million tied up in underbilling. What does that mean to the contractor's profits?

Consider this example (**TABLE 4–1**). A Wall Street approach to calculation of cost of money is based on 30 years' return

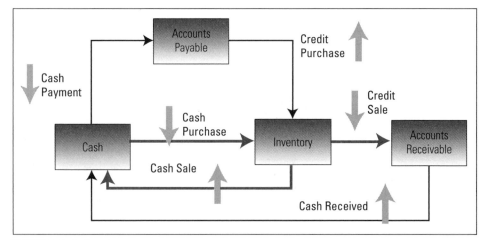

FIGURE 4–7 Cash cycle.

TABLE 4-1 Calculating the Cost of Underbilling

Cost of Underbilling	
Underbilling	$1,000,000
Cost of underbilling based on cost of money per year = $1,000,000 × 12% (30-yr average market return on investment)	$120,000
Cost of underbilling per month = $120,000 ÷ 12 (months)	$10,000
Additional monthly revenue needed to cover the cost of underbillings = $10,000 ÷ 12% gross margin	$83,000

on the stock market, which is approximately 12 percent. In other words, every month that the contractor does not have the money, he loses 1 percent of the outstanding value. One million dollars in underbilling costs $10,000 per month. How much should the contractor have to sell to recover the cost of money? Divide the $10,000 by the gross margin to get the answer. At the national average of 12 percent margin, a $10 million contractor must sell an additional $83,000 project every month just to cover the costs of underbilling.

One means of increasing cash flow is to develop a close collaboration with your distributors. Contractors believe that if they have multiple suppliers (**FIGURE 4–8**), they can work the suppliers against each other and reduce the project cost to increase the profits. Nothing can be further from the truth. Remember that distributors have to make money as well. MCA's national surveys reveal that in the best case contractors can get 1 or 2 percent better pricing on material costs overall from their suppliers. However, contractors who create a partnership with their suppliers can benefit from supplier services that reduce the 40 percent of time that their labor spends on material handling. In other words, if the distributor is willing to give discounts of 1 or 2 percent for early payments or bulk purchases, it is to your benefit to reject the discount and instead ask for the better service and delivery of the material, when, where, and how it is needed on the job site.

It is of utmost importance to remember that you must educate the distributors about the needs of the job site. Distributors

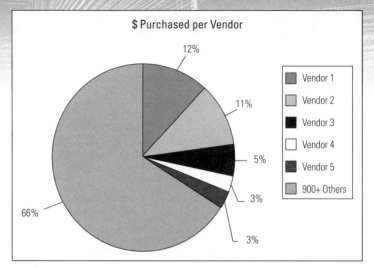

FIGURE 4–8 Sample of a contractor buying from hundreds of vendors.

often are unaware of the costs contractors carry just to process materials. For instance, MCA's research shows that on average, every purchase order (PO) written by the contractor costs $42. The cost of processing that same PO by the electrical distributor (ED) is another $72. MCA's data show that for every $10 million of sales, the contractor issues, on average, 4000 POs. In a partnership, the contractor can issue only one PO per job for commodity goods, and, by supplying the ED with the bill of material (BOM), the field can pull against the existing PO, and the PO can be updated on a regular basis.

Contractors understand that providing services adds to the distributor's costs and are willing to share the burden when it reduces their own overall costs. MCA's recent survey (**FIGURE 4–9**) indicates that the majority of contractors are willing to pay for some distributor services. The savings attained through increased productivity can substantially outweigh the direct cost of material or equipment.

Getting ECs to pay for services requires that EDs accurately quantify their organization's total costs of providing services, as well as use of the ED's resources and expertise to reduce the costs of providing such services. The cost of providing services for the electrical distributor is hidden because the resources needed to provide the services are in the fixed

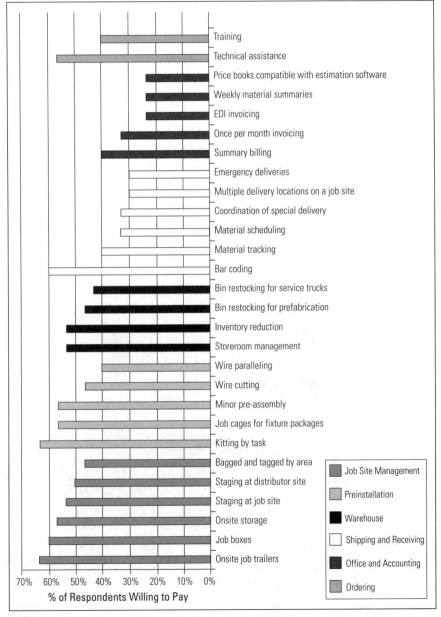

FIGURE 4–9 Contractors are willing to pay for distributor services.

category. In other words, these costs are considered to be sunk costs for distributors (**FIGURE 4–10**). Compounding the service cost issue is the fact that many services provided by the ED are lumped in with material, further masking the distributor's cost of services.

EDs cannot divide fixed costs linearly across volume of material or volume of services. Quantifying fixed resource allocation to individual services enables the most accurate pricing of services.

The biggest help you can provide to a distributor is communication and planning. By moving the customer point-of-entry forward as far as possible, distributors can use your intimate knowledge of the project to reduce their own costs. Frequently, early communication allows a distributor the flexibility to manage its own inventory and processes in such a way as to be responsive instead of reactive, while substantially reducing costs. Problems can be identified and solved before they become emergencies, further reducing costs for both parties. If a contractor insists on daily orders and receiving, the chances of having the right material at the right time for the right location is only around 63

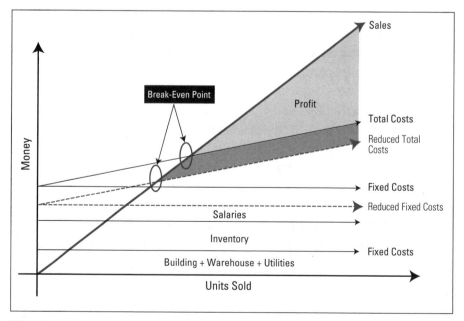

FIGURE 4–10 Improved profitability for the ED comes through reduced fixed costs.

percent (**FIGURE 4–11**). However, if the contractor orders one or two days in advance, the chance of correct material being available when needed increases by more than 30 percent.

By building a joint process of procurement, both parties can focus on their core competencies and share information in such a way as to assist the other in the areas with the most impact on profits.

By working with the distributor, you can help increase your own profitability by improving the productivity of the labor and also reducing the material cost. The ED can offer better material pricing if its costs are lowered by contractor ordering habits and planning.

Productivity and Safety

A safe job site is a productive job site. Any injury on the job site not only eliminates the injured worker's output, but also affects other workers' performance while they attend to the injured worker and afterward. Safety is not only economical but also is an emotional issue on any job site. One of the main features of an Agile job site is your ability to lay out and plan the daily, weekly, and long-term activities. Job layout and planning automatically improve safety on the job site and reduce unforeseen incidents because you avoid firefighting. Emergencies and firefighting, in other words lack of planning, are the top contributors to unsafe job sites.

The Bureau of Labor Statistics reports a 27 percent reduction in fatal and nonfatal injuries between 1992 and 2006 in the construction industry (see Appendix A). The intense attention to safety on job sites is paying off. Insurance, absenteeism, and lost time are all part of the safety picture for contractors. Collaboration between contractors, electricians, GCs, and distributors to create safe environments can help improve everyone's bottom line. In addition to the fact that a safer job site is a better work environment, safety also contributes to higher productivity. You can realize even higher benefits when the same attention that has been given to safety over the last 10 years is given to productivity as well.

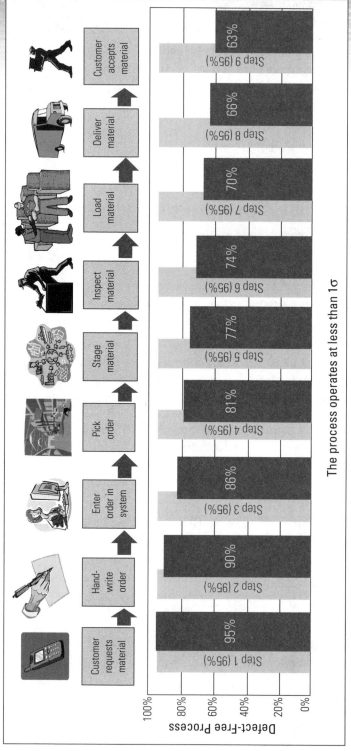

FIGURE 4-11 ED's first-time pass on EC's next-day orders.

Tools for Becoming an Agile Company

For you to be Agile, your labor needs to be Agile. For labor to be Agile, the labor needs to understand and apply the following basic skills:

- *Schedule management:* Application of Short Interval Scheduling (SIS™)
- *Procurement management:* Application of the six steps of procurement management
- *Job productivity management:* Application of Job Productivity Assurance and Control (JPAC®)

With correct understanding of these productivity tools, and how they fit into Agile Construction™, you can develop a truly productive job site. You can measurably improve profitability impacts with advance planning in each of the following areas:

- Job layout
- Project planning
- Procurement planning
- Project scheduling
- Productivity measurements
- Short interval scheduling
- Action plans for course corrections

The keys to Agility are situational awareness and visibility. When the process, the progress, and information are visible, you can ensure that activities necessary to complete the job and also run the company are better coordinated. As planning improves, both in depth and breadth, the communication bandwidth also improves (**FIGURE II–1**). A wider bandwidth of information increases the information flow between field and office.

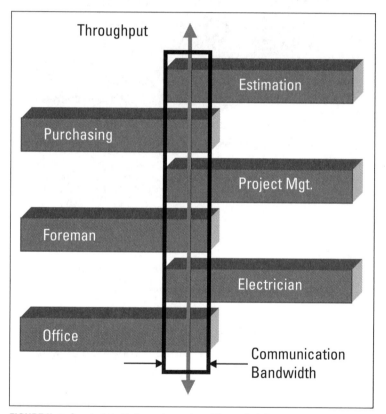

FIGURE II–1 Constraint of information and workflow principle.

Project Planning

Changes and road blocks on the job site come in every form: The general contractor (GC) changed the schedule again. You can't access the area because mechanical has not moved on. You can't install the generator because the concrete has not yet cured—and it was supposed to have been poured three weeks ago. The general is on your case to finish the termination on the second floor, but you just started because you did not have access before and just got in. The GC is pushing to finish the job and wants more workers on it, but you can't use more labor now because the new fixtures the owner wants have not yet arrived.

How often do you hear this kind of reasoning from your supervisors and foremen? Most likely, you hear it far more often than you want to. Why do these things happen? Why are electrical contractors or other subcontractors the victims of schedule changes at the last minute? Why do 90 percent of the problems show up during the last 10 percent of the job?

There is only one clear cause of chaos on the job site: lack of planning. Journeymen and wiremen in the electrical contracting industry are highly trained and will do anything to get the job done; however, they are often very cautious about making plans. The main reason they give for lack of planning is that schedules change. However, job planning is critical to their Agility as well as to the effective management of a project. With Agility, you can proactively respond to changes on the job.

Scheduling and planning serve different purposes in construction management; they are two different tools for managing jobs. You make schedules to manage change; schedules are change-management tools designed to track deviations in the job schedule from a timing, resources, and budgets point of view. Schedules vary and adjust to respond to the changing circumstances on the job site while organizing the details you need to accomplish the plan. Despite schedule variations, the plan needs to proceed.

Project plans are the road maps you use to define the design, specifications, installation, and milestones. You make plans to manage the job layout, workflow, and productivity; plans outline how the work will be accomplished. They define your expectations and goals. They do not change as often or as frequently as schedules do. When plans do change you track them with change orders that reflect the project and daily schedules. By planning, you can use knowledge to minimize risks on both the company and project levels to profitably complete the work on time and on budget.

You can see the differences between plans and schedules in the following example: Suppose you plan to travel from New York City to Seattle, Washington. This plan defines your goal, now you have to plan your means of transportation. Will you drive, take the train or bus, or fly? That decision defines your need for lodging and other amenities. Only when all the requirements and specifications have been defined can you define the milestones—when each one of the activities should take place.

When you have defined the milestones you can draft the schedule to create the scheduled plan. This schedule then becomes your change-management tool to help track any changes to the scheduled plan. If your travel dates must change, not only will the plane tickets change, but also the hotel reservations. Every day before, during, and after the trip you can add, subtract, or change the schedules to make sure that the plan happens.

Planning and scheduling for a construction project require the same elements as the trip you planned in the example. To avoid the daily chaos on the job site, the electrical contractor must have the job plan, scheduled plan, and your own schedule to comply with required milestones and deliverables. The planning process has the following structure:

- General contractor's scheduled plan (GCSP)
- Work breakdown structure (WBS)
- Electrical scheduled plan (ESP)
- Three-week scheduled plan

The following sections explain these elements in more detail.

General Contractor's Scheduled Plan

The process of job planning and scheduling starts with the general contract manager's or owner's overall job scheduled plan (**FIGURE 5–1**). The plan needs to recognize the milestones, limitations, time allocations, and deliverables that define your output as the electrical contractor. It does not have to be perfect and detailed; in fact, at the beginning of the job it needs to define only the expected delivery of the work performed by each subcontractor. You have to identify the elements of the general contractor's scheduled plan (GCSP) that affect your work.

Work Breakdown Structure

The next segment of the planning comes from building a work breakdown structure (WBS) for the project. Every electrical project has four major phases in the WBS (**FIGURE 5–2**):

- Prejob planning and layout phase
- Buying the job (procurement phase)
- Installation phase
- Closure phase

The following subsections explain these phases in more detail.

Prejob Planning and Layout Phase

FIGURE 5–3 depicts the suggested activities that you could include in the planning phase of the WBS. The activities in this phase are common activities that occur on most jobs. The process of procurement also begins in this phase; Chapter 9 of this book

Task Name	Duration	Start	Finish
Project ABC	**131 days**	**Mon 3/3/08**	**Mon 9/1/08**
Mobilize	5 days	Mon 3/3/08	Fri 3/7/08
Mobilize mechanical	30 days	Mon 3/3/08	Fri 4/11/08
Mobilize electrical	60 days	Mon 3/3/08	Fri 5/23/08
Evacuate	6 days	Mon 3/10/08	Mon 3/17/08
Formwork	7 days	Mon 3/17/08	Tue 3/25/08
Pour foundations	14 days	Tue 3/25/08	Fri 4/11/08
Steel structure	16 days	Fri 4/11/08	Fri 5/2/08
Rough-in mechanical	22 days	Fri 4/11/08	Mon 5/12/08
Form slab	7 days	Fri 5/2/08	Mon 5/12/08
Pour slab	11 days	Fri 5/9/08	Fri 5/23/08
Masonry I	11 days	Mon 5/26/08	Mon 6/9/08
Rough-in electrical	47 days	Mon 5/26/08	Tue 7/29/08
Roofing	47 days	Mon 5/26/08	Tue 7/29/08
Windows	13 days	Mon 6/9/08	Wed 6/25/08
Doors	13 days	Mon 6/9/08	Wed 6/25/08
Masonry II	19 days	Wed 6/25/08	Mon 7/21/08
Insulation	7 days	Mon 7/21/08	Tue 7/29/08
Heating	14 days	Tue 7/29/08	Fri 8/15/08
Electrical	20 days	Mon 7/21/08	Fri 8/15/08
Sanitary fittings	11 days	Mon 8/18/08	Mon 9/1/08
Paint	11 days	Mon 8/18/08	Mon 9/1/08
Completion	0 days	Sun 8/24/08	Sun 8/24/08

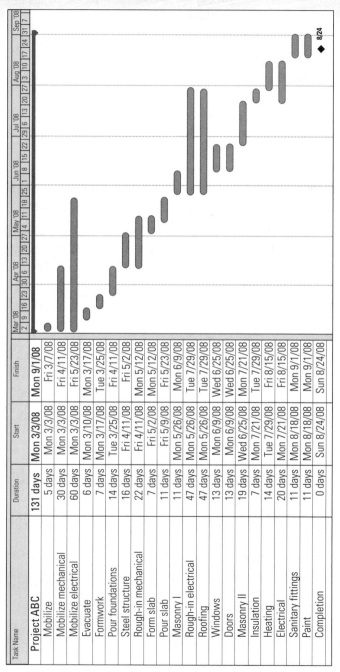

FIGURE 5-1 General contractor's scheduled plan.

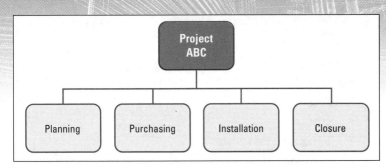

FIGURE 5–2 Four major phases of electrical jobs.

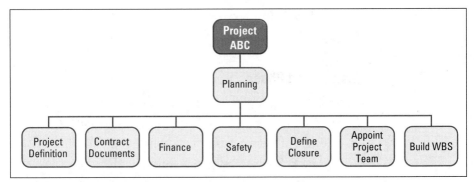

FIGURE 5–3 WBS for planning phase.

covers those steps in more detail. See Figure D-1 in Appendix D for a detailed WBS planning phase.

Buying the Job (Procurement Phase)

You must do procurement planning in the earliest phases. Purchasing is not the same as procurement; construction purchasing primarily deals with buying the material for the job. Procurement, on the other hand, includes all the activities related to the material. Material procurement planning at the onset of the job is one of the most critical parts of planning. You must plan for and track all the following issues as part of the overall project's electrical scheduled plan:

- Vendor information
- Commodity items

- Long lead time items
- Order times and frequencies
- On-site delivery
- Delivery times
- Gang boxes
- Returns
- Change orders
- Milestones
- Prefabrication
- Cut-sheets
- As-builts

FIGURE 5–4 illustrates a sample procurement plan. Figure D-2 in Appendix D shows a detailed WBS procurement phase.

Installation Phase

In the installation phase of the WBS, you break down the job into high-level cost codes and detail-level tasks. **FIGURE 5–5** shows an example of the various activities included in the installation phase of a WBS. Naturally, depending on the type of job, this portion of the WBS can vary substantially. For example, an industrial job may have a different installation breakdown than a commercial job does, and even within the commercial category a

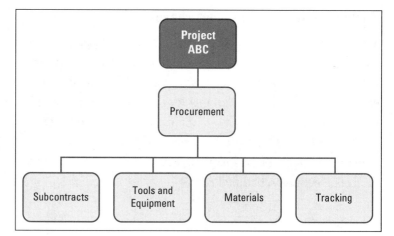

FIGURE 5–4 WBS for procurement phase.

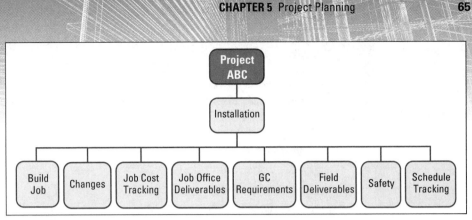

FIGURE 5–5 WBS for installation phase.

hospital may have a different breakdown than does a jail. Figure D-3 in Appendix D shows a detailed WBS installation phase.

Closure Phase

The most neglected portion of construction jobs in terms of planning is the closure. The majority of jobs in the closing phases have lost their active workforce, and even the project manager might have moved on to a new job or estimate, taking with him all the job's memory bank. Even though the steps in this phase of project planning are most common among all projects, many contractors lack a standard checklist for job completion. Holmes Electric in Seattle, Washington, developed the closure phase of the project plan depicted in **FIGURE 5–6**. Figure D-4 in Appendix D shows a detailed WBS closure phase.

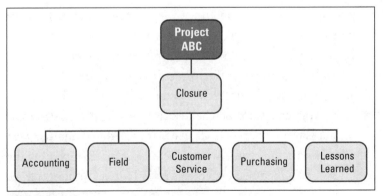

FIGURE 5–6 WBS for closure phase.
Courtesy of Holmes Electric, Inc.

Electrical Scheduled Plan

You create the electrical scheduled plan (ESP) using the WBS. Independent of the project management program used to host the project schedule, the elements of the ESP are the following:

- Project phases
- Activities under each phase
- Tasks under each activity
- Duration of each task
- Resource allocation for each task
- Cost of resources
- Material costs
- Material schedule
- Milestones—both the GC's and yours
- Schedule of values

FIGURE 5–7 is a sample schedule for all the phases and activities of a job.

Three-Week Scheduled Plan

You derive the three-week look-ahead scheduled plan from the overall electrical scheduled plan, and it works hand in hand with Short Interval Scheduling (SIS) to provide regular early warning signals of schedule changes in the project plan.

You create the three-week scheduled plan simply by filtering the tasks and activities on the electrical scheduled plan and projecting for one-, two-, and three-week periods (**TABLE 5–1**). Every time the SIS report indicates that a worker has been working on an unplanned task that is not on the three-week scheduled plan, the project manager or the field supervisor should recognize it and update the electrical scheduled plan. Even though the focus of SIS is on segregation of scheduled and unscheduled tasks, a side benefit is recognition of tasks that were scheduled but that were not placed on the three-week scheduled plan. By updating the three-week scheduled plan on a weekly basis and rolling it three weeks further, you prompt for updates of the ESP, which in turn works as an early warning signal for schedule slippage.

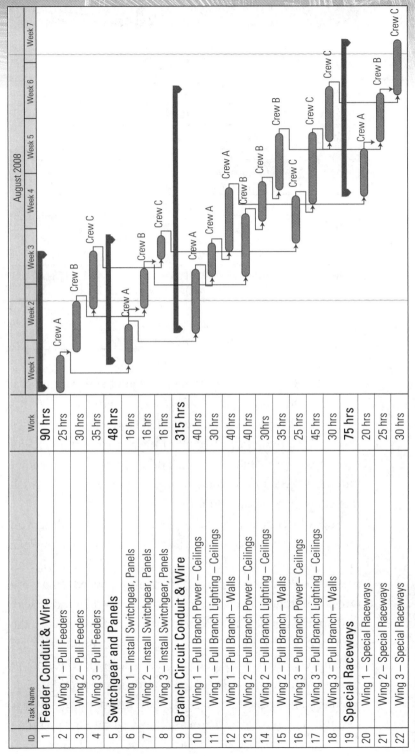

ID	Task Name	Work
1	**Feeder Conduit & Wire**	**90 hrs**
2	Wing 1 – Pull Feeders	25 hrs
3	Wing 2 – Pull Feeders	30 hrs
4	Wing 3 – Pull Feeders	35 hrs
5	**Switchgear and Panels**	**48 hrs**
6	Wing 1 – Install Switchgear, Panels	16 hrs
7	Wing 2 – Install Switchgear, Panels	16 hrs
8	Wing 3 – Install Switchgear, Panels	16 hrs
9	**Branch Circuit Conduit & Wire**	**315 hrs**
10	Wing 1 – Pull Branch Power – Ceilings	40 hrs
11	Wing 1 – Pull Branch Lighting – Ceilings	30 hrs
12	Wing 1 – Pull Branch – Walls	40 hrs
13	Wing 2 – Pull Branch Power – Ceilings	40 hrs
14	Wing 2 – Pull Branch Lighting – Ceilings	30 hrs
15	Wing 2 – Pull Branch – Walls	35 hrs
16	Wing 3 – Pull Branch Power– Ceilings	25 hrs
17	Wing 3 – Pull Branch Lighting – Ceilings	45 hrs
18	Wing 3 – Pull Branch – Walls	30 hrs
19	**Special Raceways**	**75 hrs**
20	Wing 1 – Special Raceways	20 hrs
21	Wing 2 – Special Raceways	25 hrs
22	Wing 3 – Special Raceways	30 hrs

FIGURE 5–7 Electrical scheduled plan.

TABLE 5–1 **Three-Week Scheduled Plan**		
Week 1		
Crew A	Wing 1—Pull feeders Wing 1—Install switchgear, panels	25 hrs 15 hrs
Crew B	Wing 2—Pull feeders	2.5 hrs
Week 2		
Crew A	Wing 1—Install switchgear, panels Wing 1—Pull branch power—ceilings	1 hr 39 hrs
Crew B	Wing 2—Pull feeders Wing 2—Install switchgear, panels	27.5 hrs 12.5 hrs
Week 3		
Crew A	Wing 1—Pull branch power—ceilings Wing 1—Pull branch lighting—ceilings Wing 1—Pull branch—walls	1 hr 30 hrs 9 hrs
Crew B	Wing 2—Install switchgear, panels Wing 2—Pull branch power—ceilings	3.5 hrs 36.5 hrs
Crew C	Wing 3—Pull feeders Wing 3—Install switchgear, panels Wing 3—Pull branch power—ceilings	22.5 hrs 16 hrs 1.5 hrs

FIGURE 5–8 shows the overall flow of job planning and look ahead. In addition to the feedback and feedforward of this system, the WBS also feeds into the Job Productivity Assurance and Control (JPAC), which in turn measures labor productivity and helps improve billing and cash flow. This information flows into the project and company work-in-progress (WIP), which increases the accuracy and projections.

To reduce the gap between planning and scheduling, you must create and monitor the feedback mechanism such as JPAC, SIS and other means of job measurement. By identifying all activities carried out during construction and by reducing work done on unscheduled tasks, you can increase the productivity of the job site. Job site productivity is directly related to the amount of work done according to schedule as opposed to unscheduled work or work done as filler: The higher the amount of unscheduled work done, the lower the productivity. The main reason unscheduled tasks signal a loss of productivity is because they represent the missed opportunity for planning the task accurately. When electricians are forced to work on

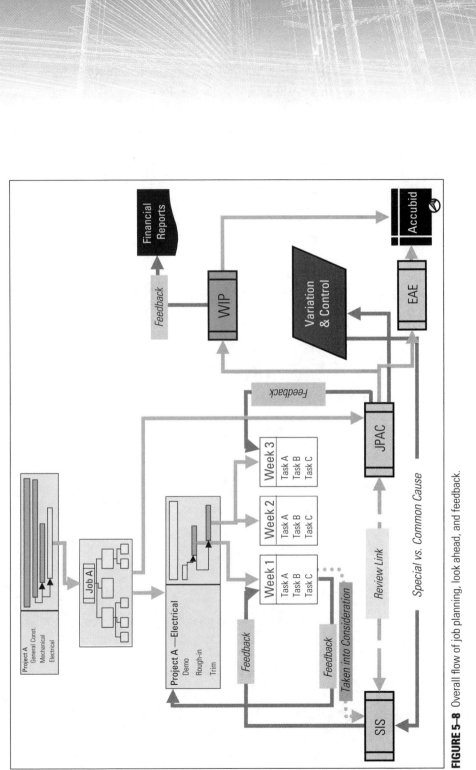

FIGURE 5-8 Overall flow of job planning, look ahead, and feedback.

unscheduled tasks, they are faced with all the issues that you have planned around for scheduled tasks: prep for installation plus relocation, lack of correct material, tools, ladders, and all items needed for installation. By tracking scheduled versus unscheduled tasks, you can identify and deal with the lost productivity attributed to the unscheduled tasks.

Operational Tools for Agility

The construction job site is very fluid and in a state of constant change. One of the main reasons for reduced productivity is that activities are invisible to the decision makers of the company. Job sites are affected by various unforeseen inside and outside factors, which makes the management of activities very difficult. To better manage the fluidity of the job site, events and changes must be made visible and traceable to managers. The tools available with Agile Construction™ make the job site and company position visible, improve the predictability of outcomes, and provide for better management of issues. All factors that negatively affect the job site must be managed, reduced, or eliminated. The tools of Agile Construction increase the visibility of the entire system, from the initial estimate through the installation and the final collection of revenue.

To take full advantage of opportunities to mitigate risk and increase profitability, you can use the following tools and processes to focus on key areas of business:

- Job Productivity Assurance and Control (JPAC®)
- Agile response to daily work changes on the job site (SIS™)
- Feedback to increase estimation accuracy and avoid "killer jobs" (EAE™)
- Improved work in progress (WIP) accuracy (See Chapter 7 for more detail on WIP)

These tools address agility needs in the following ways:

- *Enhanced system productivity.* Agile Construction focuses on improving system productivity, which relies on reduction of waste and non-value-added activity. By managing, reducing, or eliminating root causes, system productivity improves and project outcomes become much more predictable.

- *Increased estimation reliability.* You can increase the reliability of estimates by using JPAC and SIS to understand the work that occurs in the field and how that translates to job profits. Additionally, the statistical analysis of EAE takes job site factors into account, increasing the predictability and reliability of future estimates.
- *Increased visibility of the system.* Each of the tools, JPAC, SIS, EAE, and WIP, as well as the Agile processes of estimation, procurement, and project management, has an important role in the life cycle of each project, bringing visibility to daily, project, and company levels.

■ Job Productivity Assurance and Control

JPAC identifies the productivity trends of the total job, as well as the field response to individual cost codes. The graphed productivity trends model the job, enabling the contractor to visualize, monitor, and determine the root-cause of the labor variation from the field's perspective. With this insight into the job, JPAC provides the user a way to manage the causes of labor productivity variation and, ultimately, to manage the relationship between the labor productivity and job profitability.

Once a base line construction budget has been established, the work is tracked with regular and frequent updates from the field and the office. While current information comes with every update, productivity trends can be seen in just a few update cycles. JPAC projects the productivity through the end of the job based on individual cost codes, giving early warning signals regarding the outcome of the job (**FIGURE 6–1**). Data point positioning above the base line indicates the project is proceeding more productively than planned; below the base line indicates that it is less productive than planned. Even more important than the actual positioning is the trend: Is the job or cost code

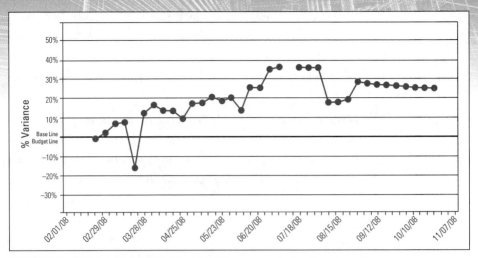

FIGURE 6–1 JPAC signaling early that the job will be more productive than planned.
Courtesy of Interstates.

becoming more or less productive as the work proceeds and the situation changes?

For example, consider the job depicted in **FIGURE 6–2** that is being tracked with JPAC. The overall job is showing a special cause variation evident in the downward trend of five consecutive points. Each point is lower than the last, which means that the expected productivity is lower and lower each week. To further identify the causes of variation in a job, segregate the job into cost codes. When you evaluate the components

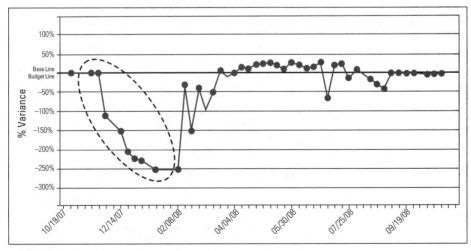

FIGURE 6–2 JPAC showing downward trend of five consecutive points.
Courtesy of TEC-Corp (Thompson Electric Company).

of this job separately (see **FIGURE 6–3**), you can clearly see that most of the job is progressing as expected except for one cost code, installation of conduit.

FIGURE 6–4 shows the productivity trend of another job. In **FIGURE 6–5**, you can see that the driving cost codes, those that severely affect the overall productivity, are conduit (raceway) and wire. However, another cost code, distribution equipment in this case, is signaling another potential problem that, if left unchecked, will affect end profitability.

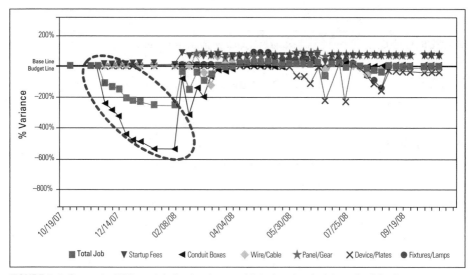

FIGURE 6–3 Cost code JPAC graph indicating that conduit is dragging the job productivity down.

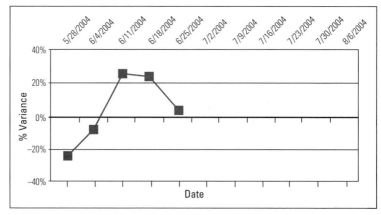

FIGURE 6–4 An overall job productivity trend tracked with JPAC.

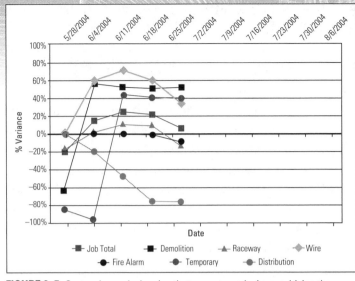

FIGURE 6–5 Cost code graph showing that raceway and wire are driving the overall productivity of the job.
Courtesy of Holmes Electric, Inc.

JPAC begins at the company level with the development of a company-wide process, the purpose of which is to build an information flow based on the monitoring of labor trends in the field.

First, you must develop a common language: a defined cost codes system of high-level "activity codes." Use these codes consistently across projects on a company-wide (or division-wide) basis. Different divisions doing other types of work may need to use a different set of cost codes, but each division should have only 15 to 20 codes. Of those, use only 7 to 10 different codes to break down any one job. JPAC tracks productivity on jobs by monitoring, and then rolling up, the productivity on the standardized cost codes.

As part of the Agile process, you can begin to use JPAC at the job planning stage by developing a work breakdown structure, or WBS, which translates a job from the estimate to the field. Initially, the project planning team segregates the job into the cost codes according to the type of work being performed. They basically create a very high-level work breakdown structure of the major activities on the job (see **FIGURE 6–6**).

At this level, it is important to develop the JPAC budget with a common understanding of the cost codes as well as consistent usage.

Tracking too few cost codes does not provide enough information to identify the source of productivity impacts. Tracking more than 10 cost codes divides the job too finely and requires excessive reporting time and tracking (see **FIGURE 6–7**) without adding valuable information.

Once you have determined the high-level cost codes for the job, along with an approximate allocation of total assigned hours from the estimate, the project management team can break down each cost code into tasks (see **TABLE 6–1**). The hours assigned to each task constitute the job budget or construction budget, which should reflect the way the technician or the operator will see the work performed. You can calculate this budget very differently from the estimate that was used to win the project.

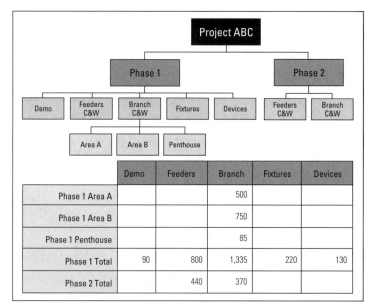

	Demo	Feeders	Branch	Fixtures	Devices
Phase 1 Area A			500		
Phase 1 Area B			750		
Phase 1 Penthouse			85		
Phase 1 Total	90	800	1,335	220	130
Phase 2 Total		440	370		

FIGURE 6–6 Setting up the high-level WBS with budgeted hours assigned to areas across the cost codes.

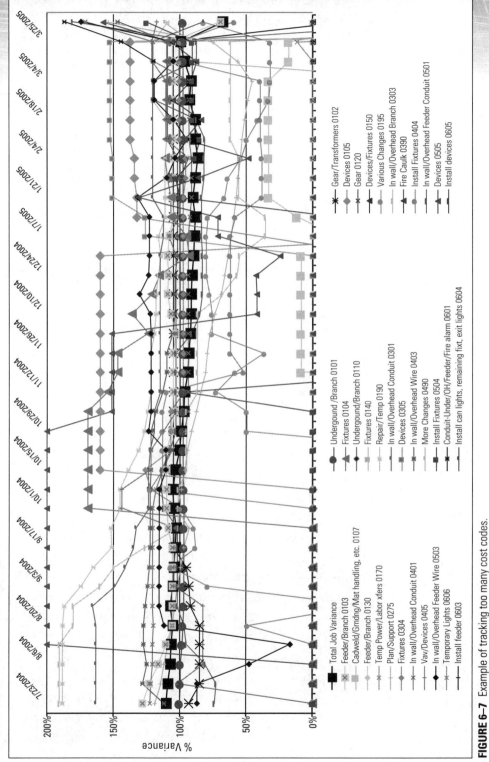

FIGURE 6–7 Example of tracking too many cost codes.

TABLE 6–1 Task Breakdown of Cost Codes That Include Base Line Budgeted Hours

	Base Line Budgeted Hours	Percentage Work for Cost Code
Phase 1 Total	90	100%
Demo Total	**90**	**100%**
Phase 1 Total	800	65%
Phase 2 Total	440	35%
Feeders Total	**1,240**	**100%**
Phase 1 Area A	500	29%
Phase 1 Area B	750	44%
Phase 1 Penthouse	85	5%
Phase 2 Total	370	22%
Branch Total	**1,705**	**100%**
Phase 1 Total	220	100%
Fixtures Total	**220**	**100%**
Phase 1 Total	130	100%
Devices Total	**130**	**100%**

The task breakdown should reflect the work in small, well-defined, measurable pieces that reflect the way the technicians view job progress. Because even the best foremen typically visualize the job only by the area that they are working on and for a maximum of 3 days in advance, the task breakdown in JPAC should be no longer than 3 to 5 days, or no longer than one update cycle in the case of a smaller job. Each task should represent visible, tangible areas, such as one room, one area, one wing, one phase, or one operation at a time. The optimal size of tasks varies with the size of the job, in both worker hours and duration, and with the number of field personnel, but less than 500 hours or 5 percent of the job is often a reasonable starting point.

On the job, technicians report the observed percentage complete for each task that they work on during the update period. Compare these completed percentages with the high-level cost code labor hours submitted weekly for payroll. If the observed completion is outpacing the planned hours, the job is deemed to be ahead and therefore more productive.

Additionally, with JPAC you can forecast productivity to the end of the job, assuming that the job proceeds at the current level of productivity in each cost code. By drilling down to see trending at the cost code level, you can identify the sources of the variation in the JPAC graph. First, look at the trending of the cost code level graphs, and second, correlate the variation to the data provided by the SIS.

On any job, two to four costs codes, for example, pipe, wire, branch, and fixture, generally drive cost codes that encompass the majority of the work.

The job shown in **FIGURE 6-8** was tracked with JPAC. The overall job shows the influence of a special cause, evidenced by the extreme points. By drilling down to examine the job at a cost code level, you can clearly identify the cost codes affecting the productivity decline. Because the job is no longer proceeding according to plan, the profits will no longer be earned according to plan.

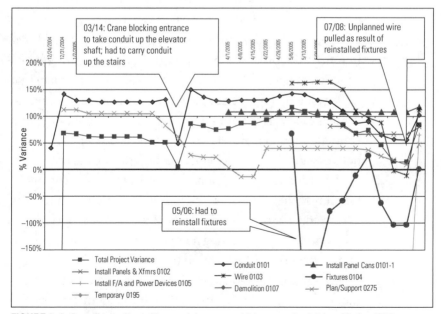

FIGURE 6-8 Overall job affected by special causes, which are made visible with the JPAC cost code graph.

Typically, on a weekly basis, technicians report the Observed Percent Complete of each task. You can then compare these completed percentages with the hours turned in to accounting and track on a weekly basis. This observed percentage completed takes into account the difficulty of installation and is a measure of system productivity. The foreman reports percentage complete of the work, not the hours or the portion of material installed, for each task. If the hours used are lower than the percentage complete, the job is deemed to be ahead of schedule and therefore more productive.

For true agility, you must understand and use productivity and trend monitoring measurements. Both JPAC and SIS use trend monitoring and the science behind statistical process control (SPC) so that you can make an appropriate and timely Agile response to the ever-changing conditions of the job site. In both cases, you measure the job, task, or project against a base line construction budget in JPAC, and the scheduled tasks in SIS.

■ Special Causes versus Common Causes

Although you might see the effects of variation every day on the job, you must analyze the causes and magnitude of the deviation from the plan to apply the correct strategy. All too often contractors have a costly knee-jerk reaction to a problem that is the result of the system, not an event with an individual trigger that can be fixed with a temporary solution. For example, a contractor reorders material because the original material cannot be found. This causes labor wastage during the time when the labor is waiting for the new material to arrive. The misallocation of the material on the job site may be a symptomatic management issue rather than a one-time problem. Solving this problem simply by ordering more material hides the real cause of material mismanagement on the job site.

To reduce variation appropriately, first you must analyze the underlying source of the variation to determine whether it is a special cause with an identifiable external influence or a common cause, an inherent result of the process. In many cases, the reason for a certain outcome is not obvious. For example, a material order was placed for far more material than was budgeted for the job. In response, the contractor institutes a policy that every order must be approved and signed for at three levels: on the job site, with project management, and by an executive. However, the excessive material order might have resulted from an order for 10 panels that was mistakenly transcribed as 70 because of unreadable handwriting or became 100 because of a sticky key during data entry. If variations are the result of such one-time or infrequent issues, they are special cause variations, and the cost of a new policy, in this case obtaining executive approval on material needed in the field, far outweighs the benefits, in this case the effort of implementing a field-based ordering system. On the other hand, the excessive material order could be a result of the system, for example, the material must be onsite to develop an appropriate billing schedule, or the supplier rewards large orders with a generous return policy so that project managers regularly build a buffer into their orders. Errors and behaviors that occur over and over are common cause variations, and parts of the system needs to be redesigned or improved, in this case this can be done through implementing electronic purchase orders or a confirmation process.

To distinguish special cause variation from common cause variation, you must make the variation visible. JPAC and SIS make field labor productivity and impacts visible. Once the variation is visible, you can use the trends to evaluate the underlying source. Special cause variation requires immediate intervention, and system-level causes (called common cause variation) can only be affected by improving the entire system.

You can see common cause variation as an irregular series of small ups and downs driven by the system and its processes (see **FIGURE 6–9**). There is not a single identifiable cause—the ups and downs show the combined effect of a multitude of inter-

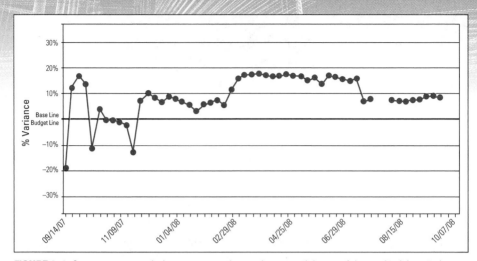

FIGURE 6–9 Common cause variation appears as the regular ups and downs of the productivity trend.

related or unrelated causes. For example, the material shows up anywhere between 10:00 a.m. and noon; three or four electricians are no-shows today; 10 to 15 percent of needed items are backordered; the safety meeting takes between 15 minutes and an hour; it might snow. If nothing changes in how the process operates in the near future, you can predict the range of possible outcomes with high confidence. The smaller the range of the possible outcomes, the more predictable the outcome; the wider the range, the less predictable it becomes.

Special cause variation, on the other hand, occurs not simply by chance influences but as the result of a (or several) specific outside influence. For example, the ground froze, so the concrete wasn't poured and therefore the electricians couldn't get in to set the hangers. The delivery truck broke down, causing the distributor to miss the stop at the job site. The foreman scheduled to be on the job today was called to an emergency on another job site. These types of one-time occurrences appear in the trends, showing that something special, whether good or bad, happened on a particular day.

If these are regular occurrences, the signals do not appear in the trends. For example, if the foreman is called away frequently, this does not appear as a disruption in stark contrast to the regular flow of the job as it would if the foreman is regularly on the job site. If the distributor regularly arrives at 8:30 a.m. and once shows up at 2:00 p.m. instead, you can easily see the impact of the late arrival. Reacting too quickly to common cause variation by treating it as though it were a special cause is costly and nonproductive. Not reacting to special cause variation is also costly because you allow the situation to go undetected or without management.

Case Studies

Thompson Electric Company (TEC) of Sioux City, Iowa, has been using JPAC for more than 3 years. The learning process that TEC had to go through is very common among companies learning to apply this Agile tool. **FIGURE 6–10** shows one of the early JPAC graphs for TEC. The project managers and foremen had to decide what cost codes they would use and start the tracking. The initial issues surfaced when activities that were not related to installation but reported under various cost codes

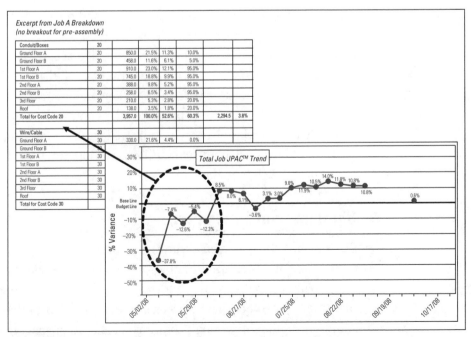

FIGURE 6–10 Early Thompson Electric JPAC, where noninstallation activities were not reported
Courtesy of TEC-Corp (Thompson Electric Company).

drove the productivity below planned budget. Within a few weeks, it became obvious that, for example, if the labor was working on prepping the fixtures and allocated their time to the fixture cost code, but no progress in installation was observed, the fixture cost code would appear negative. It was not until the project manager included the preassembly as part of the cost code activity that the job progress started and productivity started to stabilize.

TABLE 6–2 shows a more recent job, which takes into account all the cost code–related activities. By using JPAC on all their jobs, TEC is a very productive and profitable company. In most companies, the definition, understanding, and usage of cost codes vary between project managers and foremen. By using common tools and tracking systems such as JPAC, TEC was able to create a common understanding among the field labor and PMs about the cost code definitions and usage.

By using JPAC, Holmes Electric Company (HEC) of Seattle, Washington, also discovered that cost codes do not always mean the same thing to everyone. By creating clear and precise definitions, a cross-functional team that included estimation, field personnel, project management, purchasing, and accounting, standardized the usage of the cost codes throughout the company. HEC's application of JPAC on a very large commercial job under a guaranteed maximum pricing (GMP) contract ensured correct tracking of the job despite the limited scope designed at the beginning of the job. **FIGURE 6–11** shows the job turnaround to productivity and profitability.

■ Short Interval Scheduling

SIS, or Short Interval Scheduling, is a foreman's schedule, established and measured by the foreman on a short-term basis. With SIS, you can carry out your plans for productivity by bringing together the materials and labor needed in the short term while supporting a coordinated effort of managing all the aspects of the job plan. With SIS progress reporting, you can identify and quantify the actual productive work on

Job #123, Hotel ABC Foreman: Les Ballard Project Mgr: Kevin Lytle	Cost Code	Budgeted Hours	% Work for Cost Code	% Work for Job	Observed Completion %	Accounting Hours	Variance
Temporary Power	**80**						
Temp Power	80	120.0	100.0%	1.0%	98.0%		
Total for Cost Code 80		**120.0**	**100.0%**	**1.0%**	**98.0%**	**113.0**	**3.9%**
Systems	**100**						
1st-Floor Assembly	100	250.0	6.0%	2.1%	100.0%		
2nd-Floor Assembly	100	500.0	11.9%	4.2%	100.0%		
3rd-Floor Assembly	100	500.0	11.9%	4.2%	100.0%		
4th-Floor Assembly	100	500.0	11.9%	4.2%	100.0%		
1st-Floor Install	100	350.0	8.3%	3.0%	100.0%		
2nd-Floor Install	100	700.0	16.7%	5.9%	100.0%		
3rd-Floor Install	100	700.0	16.7%	5.9%	100.0%		
4th-Floor Install	100	700.0	16.7%	5.9%	100.0%		
Total for Cost Code 100		**4,200.0**	**100.0%**	**35.5%**	**100.0%**	**2,239.0**	**46.7%**
Fire Alarm Systems	**110**						
1st Floor	110	92.0	32.1%	0.8%	0.0%		
2nd Floor	110	65.0	22.6%	0.5%	50.0%		
3rd Floor	110	65.0	22.6%	0.5%	95.0%		
4th Floor & Roof	110	65.0	22.6%	0.5%	95.0%		
Total for Cost Code 110		**287.0**	**100.0%**	**2.4%**	**54.4%**	**187.0**	**-19.9%**

TABLE 6-2 TEC JPAC Breakdown with Budgets and Reporting on Assembly and Installation Activities

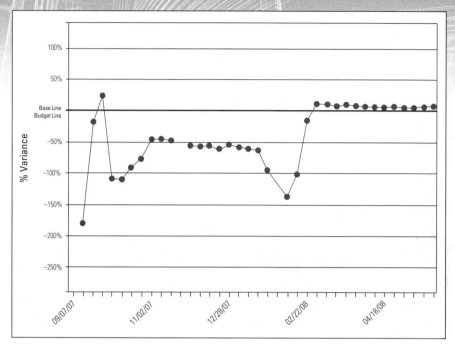

FIGURE 6–11 Holmes Electric application of JPAC helped identify issues early on so that they could be resolved to ensure productivity on a critical guaranteed maximum price contract.
Courtesy of Holmes Electric, Inc.

the job so that you can better manage the cash flow, labor, and materials.

As with JPAC, SIS uses trend monitoring and the science behind statistical process control (SPC) so that you can take appropriate and timely action. The reasons for lost productivity become visible, unmasking the job's true requirements for performing the work. The foreman and the project manager can use this information to improve the system-level causes of lost productivity, revenue, and profits.

In SIS, the operator (electrician or foreman) is simply asked to schedule his or her work for the next 3 days. The schedule is then scored by the project manager on a daily basis, with deviations from the schedule identified by a cause. (See **TABLE 6–3**.)

First, the foreman establishes a look ahead to determine which tasks that contribute to the completion of the project the crew will work on over the next few days (**TABLE 6–4**). This form is used to capture the activities that the foreman is planning for

TABLE 6-3 Sample Short Interval Schedule

Day	Task	Scheduled Time	Percentage Complete	Reason for < 100% Completion	Number of Scheduled Hours Lost

Reason Codes (Why Couldn't I Complete My Schedule?):
1. Other contractors in the way
2. Weather
3. Not having material when we need it; not having the right material
4. Material ordering practices
5. Not having rental equipment in the place we need it
6. Manpower—getting the guys on site
7. Manpower—having appropriate skill level
8. Preparing areas for other contractors or our own subs (not known ahead of time)
9. Waiting for other subs
10. Engineering design—design not done
11. Other:

TABLE 6–4   Example of Short Interval Schedule for a Specific Project

Day	Task	Scheduled Time	Percentage Complete	Reason for < 100% Completion	Number of Scheduled Hours Lost
Monday 10/27/2008	Upper-Level Framing Rough-In Grid C-D Site Work—Underground Telecom Conduit Upper-Level Audio/Video Conduit Rough-In	Bob 8 hrs Rudy 3 hrs Rudy 5 hrs			
Tuesday 10/28/2008	Upper-Level Framing Rough-In Grid A-C Site Work—Underground Telecom Conduit Upper-Level Lighting Rough-In Grid D-F	Bob 8 hrs Rudy 3 hrs Rudy 5 hrs			
Wednesday 10/29/2008	Upper-Level Framing Rough-In Grid D-F Site work—Underground Telecom Conduit	Bob 5 hrs Bob 3 hrs Rudy Off			

the crew for each day for the next 3 days. The foreman looks ahead 3 days to answer the following questions:

1. What needs to be done?
2. Who will be doing the tasks?
3. How many hours do the electricians need to complete the task?

In addition to the tasks, the foreman can also use the SIS form to schedule for tools and material by answering the following questions:

4. Do the workers have all the material they need?
5. Are the tools in operational form and in place?
6. Is any prefabrication needed for their tasks?

The foreman fills out this form and hands it out to the electricians each day. At the end of the day, the foreman collects the forms and answers a few more questions:

7. What did the electricians do today?
8. Were the tasks finished as scheduled?
9. What obstacles prevented tasks from being completed as scheduled?
10. If the electricians could not finish their tasks, did they do something else?
11. Which tasks did they do in place of the scheduled ones?

To make the scoring easier for the foreman, create a list of potential obstacles at the beginning of the job.

By evaluating the foreman's responses to the preceding questions, the project manager can accurately predict material and worker needs, track the project plan, and improve the bandwidth of communication between everyone involved in the project.

Depending on the company, the leading cause of failure to comply with the short-term schedule could come from a number of areas: trade interference, rework, insufficient information, or design changes to the job. However, often the most frequently heard complaint from the field is that the materials are not available. SIS shows that this is a side effect, a direct result of working on a different task from the scheduled task, rather than the cause of lost productivity.

The project manager can objectively separate the real cause from the apparent cause. For example, if the crew was forced to work in a different area, the immediately apparent cause may have been that the materials were unavailable, but the underlying cause was that the crew was forced to change their schedule and work on different tasks after they were mobilized to work on the planned tasks. SIS data as shown in **FIGURE 6–12** identifies the actual waste in the field, recognizing the portion of work that is not productive and assigning a value to it; for example, SIS can identify the 27 percent of the time going to rework that cannot be seen in the accounting measures, or the 10 percent of the hours lost to waiting for other trades to free an area.

The ripple effects from the increased visibility carry throughout the company. Furthermore, you can determine which types of work and in which situations the company can perform most predictably so that you are in a much stronger position through the entire process, from identifying profitable types of work, to estimating costs correctly, to managing manpower and materials profitably on the job.

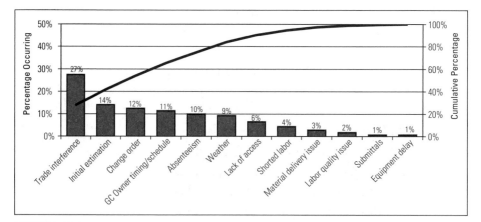

FIGURE 6–12 Results of collecting SIS feedback on four projects over four months.

Case Study

Next to material handling, unscheduled work is the highest contributor to loss of labor productivity on the job site. Even if the labor does something else instead of the scheduled task, the time it takes to demobilize and remobilize for each activity can be as large as the task itself and becomes lost and unrecoverable hours for the contractor, leading to a smaller proportion of productive hours used by the labor.

Holmes Electric Company (HEC) of Seattle used SIS to identify unforeseen obstacles in their labor productivity. **TABLE 6–5** shows the simple SIS form HEC used to track unscheduled time due to the issues on the job site out of HEC's control. The resulting Pareto chart, a chart that ranks the highest to lowest negative impact on job schedule (**FIGURE 6–13**), depicts the

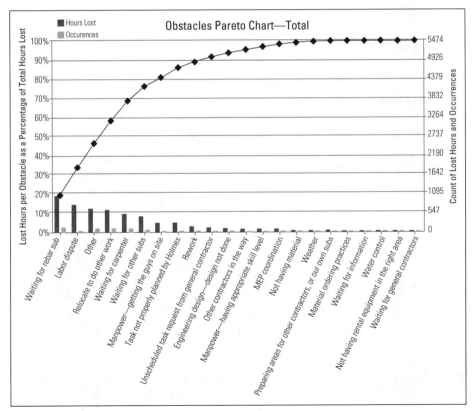

FIGURE 6–13 Results of using SIS to track impacts to the schedule on one project.
Courtesy of Holmes Electric, Inc.

TABLE 6-5 HEC Example of SIS

Day	Task	Scheduled Time	Percentage Complete	Reason for < 100% Completion	Number of Scheduled Hours Lost
8/09	Terminate motors field Finish field side	3 guys 3 motors .5 day	0%	2	.5 day
	Terminate start motors MCC side	3 guys 3 motors .5 day	200%		
8/10	Finish terminate MCC side	2 guys .5 day	done 8/09		
	Terminate DFC cabinet	2 guys .5 day			
	Terminate controls	1 guy 1 day	50% 8/09		
8/11	Hang lights pumphouse Bond all pipes Fix lighting outdoor fixtures	1 guy 1 day 1 guy .5 day 1 guy .5 day			

Reason Codes (Why Couldn't the Schedule Be Completed?):
 1. Other contractors in the way
 2. Weather
 3. Not having material when we need it; not having the right material
 4. Material ordering practices
 5. Not having rental equipment in the place we need it
 6. Manpower—getting the guys on site
 7. Manpower—having appropriate skill level
 8. Preparing areas for other contractors or our own subs (not known ahead of time)
 9. Waiting for other subs
10. Engineering design—design not done
11. Other:

amount and frequency of lost scheduled time, which lead to lower productivity. By addressing root causes, HEC was able to keep their labor focused on the productive scheduled work.

Agile Procurement

The goal of Agile procurement is to reduce job site material handling and other waste rather than reduce the cost of material. For this reason, you should select suppliers based on what they can do to provide the correct material, at the installation location, prepared to be installed, at the time that the labor is ready to install it. The tradeoff for increased productivity is worth a higher price on the material if the cost includes such labor productivity–increasing services as these:

- Specification verification
- Submittal preparation support
- Receiving, inspection, and damage claims support
- Offsite storage at the vendor's secure warehouse
- Preassembly of selected components
- Wire cutting and paralleling
- Testing of equipment
- Kitting and packaging in job packs suitable for installation
- Staged deliveries to the job site, delivering as the material is needed
- Stocking and maintaining onsite boxes and trailers for commodity materials
- Material returns processing
- Job site material clean-off

Part III of this book discusses the process of procurement for Agile Construction in more detail. To use material procurement as an Agile tool, you must focus on the value of the material versus the worker-hours needed to manage that material. The lost worker-hours in receiving, handling, returning, moving, and storing the material often is much more expensive than the potential savings from early purchases and payments. The cost of labor spent on material handling could be as high as 40 percent of the total labor used for the job.

You can implement various methods to help the labor reduce time spent handling material. For example, consider the following issues when you establish job site delivery for the Agile procurement process:

- Location of delivery by vendors or third-party carriers
- Manpower required to unload trucks and who will provide the manpower
- Types and quantity of equipment needed to move material on the job site and who will provide or arrange for the equipment
- Procedures to deal with delays and changes after the material has been delivered
- Process exceptions and variations that will be needed to accommodate errors and other emergency material needs

Job site material movement can be highly subjective and is usually based on the foremen's and installers' experiences with the vendors. For example, foremen who are consistently plagued with backorders and incorrect material tend to order more than they need, or they may even order for the entire project at the beginning and feel more comfortable with the fact they have enough material to work any plan that becomes necessary.

Simple solutions to material flow can help improve labor productivity and reduce labor waste. For example, on a large job, having a trailer managed by the distributor can help reduce material multihandling. **FIGURE 6–14** shows a job site trailer manned and managed by Graybar Electric in Atlanta, Georgia. If the job is small or requires smaller commodity goods placed in various locations at the site, a gang box management program in collaboration with the supplier can help reduce both labor and material wastage (see **FIGURE 6–15**). In addition to any kind of vendor-managed inventory, you can use lower-cost labor to manage the material on the job site. In a very large high-rise complex, Holmes Electric Company uses up to seven unindentured electricians under a very experienced supervisor to reduce the time their 80-man workforce spends on material handling. If they would have managed the job in the traditional way, they

FIGURE 6–14 Vendor-managed job site trailer.
Courtesy of Graybar.

FIGURE 6–15 Photo of a vendor-managed gang box on a job site.
Courtesy of Graybar.

would have had 80 highly paid electricians doing the job of the seven lower-paid helpers in addition to their other work.

Case Study

Interstates Electrical Company of Sioux Center, Iowa, applied Agile procurement to help them reduce their labor costs on three comparable jobs more than 30 percent. **FIGURE 6–16** and **BOX 6–1** show the labor reduction and cost savings. **FIGURE 6–17** shows clamshells used as buffers for common material on these jobs.

In a different case, the vendor-assembled fixtures were delivered in mesh-type gang boxes to the location for installation

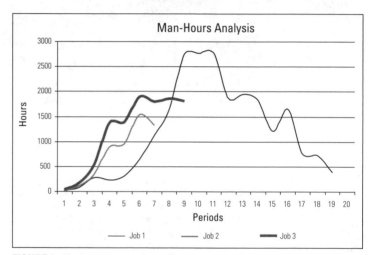

FIGURE 6–16 Results of using Agile procurement to reduce manpower peak. Courtesy of Interstates.

BOX 6–1 Comparison of Projects in Figure 6–16

- All are 30-million-gallon industrial plants
- All three jobs have same owner
- All material supplied by Van Meter
- Three different project managers
- Same contract value
- Job 1 = 0% Agile
- Job 2 = 75% Agile
- Job 3 = 100% Agile
- Job 2 and Job 3 will not add any more men, will not change the work schedule (45 hr/week)

FIGURE 6–17 Using clamshells as buffers for common materials.
Courtesy of Graybar.

on a job in Atlanta, Georgia. The contractor, Cleveland Electric Company, in partnership with Graybar Electric, was able to line up their forces for better productivity (see **FIGURE 6–18**).

Estimation Analysis Enhancement

Estimators must always try to learn from their experiences and correct the estimation labor units for the next job. The correction must come from outside information. Did we lose the bid? Did we get the bid and lose the profits? Did we encounter a "killer job" that cost us far more to complete than we earned on other jobs combined? Are bids going out with sales numbers supported by the local market? Are cost estimates identifying what it will take for us to do the work?

This level of questioning is preliminary, but extremely important. However, this approach to estimation is a risk-adverse approach that has as much chance to win a job with a high profit as it has to land a killer job. The estimator must use information to build the correction factors for the next job. If the correction factors come solely from previous bids and the final accounting

FIGURE 6–18 Vendor-assembled fixtures helped improve labor productivity on this project.
Courtesy of Graybar.

numbers, the estimator misses the most important factor on the next job: how do we do at this kind of work?

Because the estimator's correction factor comes from the field, if the field data are erroneous, the correction factor for the next job is also erroneous. For example, if branch wiring is considered to be a problem cost code when it has more than 20 percent of the job's total hours, the estimator adds extra cushion to cover the risk. Naturally, these kinds of tactics are not hidden from the field labor. When the field labor knows there is an extra cushion in the branch cost code, they respond by using it as their own cushion, dumping any uncoded time or overages into this cost code. Suddenly, that cost code looks bad, and on every job. Then, the estimator takes this signal as vindication that he was right—the company does not perform well in branch—and keeps adding more hours to the branch or avoids jobs with high percentage of branch as their total labor hours. This tailspin continues until the estimates become uncompetitive or killer jobs eat all the hard-earned profits from all other jobs. On the other hand, if the company does well on the branch on the next job because of an overlarge cushion or because the field labor allocates miscellaneous work differently, the estimator may respond with a swing in the opposite direction.

You can view the accuracy of estimation in construction from two different perspectives. One is accounting or "exactness accuracy"; the other is "job-related performance-based accuracy." The initial estimate calls for 2 hours per fixture, or a total of 200 hours. (See **TABLE 6–6**.) At the end of the week, the electrician reports that he has installed eight fixtures and burned through 16 hours on that task. Using a typical accounting report, the estimator would conclude that the progress is on target. Sixteen hours divided by the eight fixtures installed is 2 hours per fixture. But suppose the first four fixtures take 2 hours to install. Then, because of an improved learning curve, fixture number 5 takes only 1 hour and numbers 6 and 7 are installed in 1.5 hours total. Fixture number 8, unexpectedly, but for many of the reasons identified earlier, takes 4 hours to install (See Figure 2–5). How does the job's outcome look now? Will the rest of the job proceed like the first four fixtures and meet the estimation

TABLE 6–6 **Estimated vs. Actual Fixture Installation Reporting**			
• 100 fixtures to install • Estimated at 2 hours per fixture • 8 fixtures have been installed			
	Estimate	**To Date**	**Remaining**
Labor	200 hr	16 hr	184 hr
Labor Cost @ $50 loaded	$10,000	$800	$9,200
Material Cost @ $100 each	$10,000	$10,000	$0

budget while hiding the installation difficulties? Or will the rest proceed like fixtures number 5 and 6, making money through better than expected productivity, or like fixture 8, sinking the entire cost code and potentially the entire job? Without field input, it is anyone's guess. Knowing labor productivity and issues helps improve the estimation accuracy of Agile contractors.

When precision of the estimate is simply a matter of the estimator taking the time and reviewing the specs and drawings to arrive at the correct count of material, this is termed job-performance-based accuracy. The smallest improvement in job-performance-based estimation accuracy can lead to significant improvement in profitability. By recognizing the importance of job-performance-based estimation, using available data from estimation, using accounting and the field to determine labor units, and creating a useful tool for making decisions based on the historic performance, you can improve estimation accuracy and profitability.

Data Analysis to Improve Estimation Accuracy

In football, a catastrophic loss does not go unstudied. Although one player may have missed a critical pass, or another committed an unnecessary penalty, without going back and reviewing the whole game tape, the team runs the risk of encountering the same outcome in the next game. In football, the coach doesn't say, "We lost to them before, so we won't play them again," yet that is often the response in construction: "We can't go after this kind of job or work with this GC or for that owner because we lost money doing it before."

In football, the team reviews the tapes, evaluates the statistics, and looks for opportunities to develop the team's performance. The important fact is not that the team lost, but why they lost and how they can avoid letting it happen the next time. For example, if they came up short on defense in every game last season, the same thing will continue to happen unless the team takes steps to build the defense. This information must be fed back to the team. If the team takes the required steps to remedy the deficiency, whether through increased training, strategy changes, or personnel changes, the coaches need to use those data in addition to the historical data to make predictions for the upcoming season; history alone is no longer the best predictor. The same should be true in construction job estimating: Without reliable historical data that capture job performance and recognition of current development and performance, the celebration on bid day could evolve into a catastrophe on the job site in a few short months.

In a football game, painful losses usually occur when a team (including coaches) is not well prepared, both strategically and tactically. The pregame studies did not foreshadow what they encountered on game day. The same is true in construction: If the historical job-based data are not used during estimation to model the job, there is far greater risk of the job becoming a killer job.

Estimating without historic data is like operating without a long-term memory. You may remember what you ate for dinner last night, but, unless you eat exactly the same thing every night or had a special meal on a particular occasion, you likely do not remember exactly what you ate on February 23 or July 17 or November 3. The same thing happens in construction: You see the final numbers and remember how the job ended. You might remember a notable missed delivery or project change, but you probably do not remember the hundreds of other ups and downs that led to the final numbers.

Averages of the job do not provide a clear picture of what happened from the estimate to the closeout. The first step for improving estimation accuracy is to compile and analyze historical data by cost code and specific job characteristics. Once the data analysis is established, the estimators can improve the job-based estimation accuracy further by focusing on improving the quality of the data through an accurate measure of job productivity.

The first step in data mining is to use the available data from estimation and accounting to compare estimated to actual profits. There is an implicit understanding in the industry of "acceptable" profit based on historical averages. **FIGURE 6–19** shows the estimated profits for a real set of jobs. Note that each estimate predicts a gross profit return between 12 percent and 24 percent, well in line with the industry averages of 12–14 percent, according to the latest figures from the Construction Financial Management Association (CFMA). The reality, however, is somewhat different. At the end of these jobs, the actual profits varied anywhere from a 41 percent gain to a 12 percent loss.

Why the difference? Estimators typically work with an average performance of the cost codes, or even the average performance of the jobs, over time. However, using averages of data without considering the range and statistical outliers skews the results. To use the available data correctly, estimators must consider factors such as geography, cost code mix, allowance for preassembly, and type of construction to make confident decisions based on more than just averages.

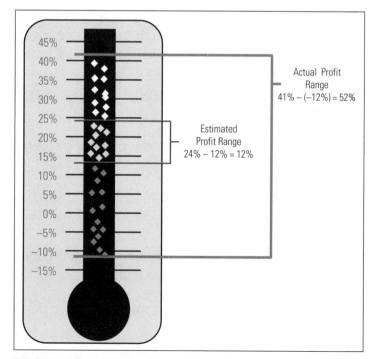

FIGURE 6-19 Typical EC job-to-job variability in profitability.

For example, if an estimator looks at how a job turned out, he or she may see something like the graph shown in **FIGURE 6–20**. The job was completed in fewer hours than were estimated, but approximately on target. However, the cost code comparisons in **FIGURE 6–21** show that the job's "average" hours do not show the entire picture. Some cost codes were underestimated, some were overestimated, each to varying degrees. If the next estimate has a majority of hours in cost code 402, the job could be very profitable for the contractor. However, if the next job up for bid is one with a lot of hours in cost code 302, the contractor could be dealing with a killer job.

Beyond cost codes, other anomalies and clues might also be hidden unless the data are segregated correctly and compared with similar jobs. Certain shared characteristics such as the job location, type of work, customer type, and contract type can also provide insight into the way that a cost code is handled and reported from the field. Using data that accurately represents the work environment adds more detail to the estimation process and allows for more selective bidding.

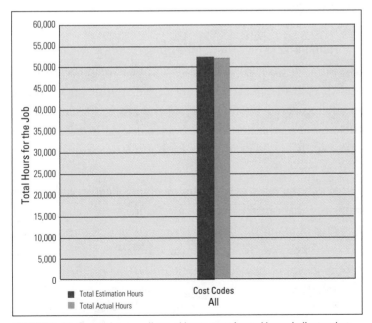

FIGURE 6–20 Comparing overall actual hours to estimated hours indicates that the job is doing well.

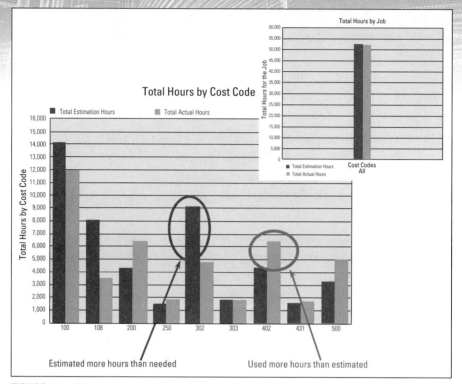

FIGURE 6–21 Comparing estimated hours to actual hours by cost codes shows a different picture.

FIGURE 6–22 shows the same cost code comparisons across several jobs, measuring the difference between the estimate and the performance. The data reveal significant variation in the expected productivity of the labor, depending, in this case, on whether the job was managed from the home office with local labor and whether it was new work or a renovation.

When the job was local and one type of construction, this company's historical estimating procedures were a good indicator of the outcome on the job. However, when the same job type occurred in a remote location, the estimate overcompensated for the location. In a second type of job, the estimates in two separate cost codes were in no way a match for the job site. **TABLE 6–7** reveals the results of the study, indicating cost code productivity variation.

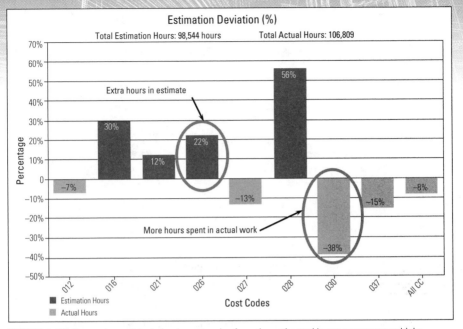

FIGURE 6–22 Comparison of deviation in cost codes from the estimated hours across several jobs.

Another example is the mobilization and demolition cost codes, which show a sharp difference from the original estimate to the field performance depending on the job's location and the type of construction. The contractor would have not discovered this result if the jobs were measured only on their production output instead of on their productivity. In this contractor's case, the majority of the work the company has done historically is new work or local work; the company takes a big risk by estimating a renovation job in a new area. The contractor's overall average historical labor figures are not a good indicator of this distant renovation job. In this case, an across-the-board response to the negative impact of the two cost codes shown as demolition and fixtures would have had the result of damaging the currently predictable type 1 (local new construction) jobs. By recognizing that the accounting data were actually the result of a productivity response to a different situation, the company was able to better evaluate the job site needs of this particular type of work.

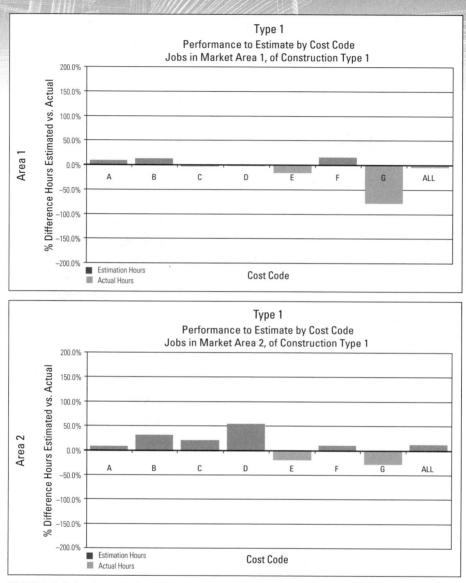

TABLE 6–7 Estimation deviations across geography and type of work. *(Continues)*

Accounting Feedback to Estimation

Estimation has a twofold role in any construction company. First, pricing the work for the market, a sales role, and second, identifying the probable costs associated with completing the installation. The company's financial outcome on any job, although actually determined on the job site, is predicted

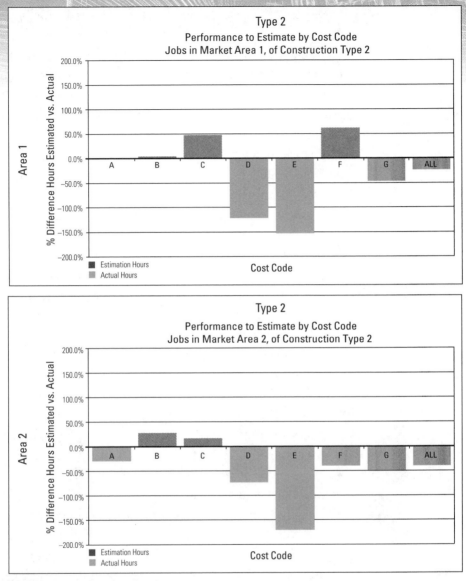

TABLE 6–7 *(Continued)*

during the estimation. No company can afford to take on killer jobs.

Using the previous example, the contractor historically has had poor performance in fixture installation regardless of location. On the new local jobs, data show they typically finish 30 percent over budget on hours used versus estimated hours. A bid comes in that the company wants to take a risk on, so the estimators bid the job tight. If the estimator does not realize that the average of 30 percent over budget becomes an average loss of 170 percent in the case of renovation construction, and this upcoming bid is for a renovation job, the job can become a killer instantly. Even if it is known that a particular cost code is a dumping ground for hours, the data are still valuable because they reflect how the field uses the cost codes. This difference needs to be understood. The measurements may be valid, but may not measure exactly what was intended.

You can enhance the analysis of data for estimation accuracy by improving the quality, depth, and categorization of the data. When only certain jobs are reported or included, the next estimate can be made only on those data. The same is true in football: Game tapes are of limited value if they include only the first half, the final minute, or high-profile games. Improved job-based data come from better recognition and measurement of the actual events in the field as the construction is put in place. The closer the measurement is to the actual work, the more useful it is as input to the estimation process.

You should analyze the job data carefully. Identifying the outlier data is very critical to the correct analysis of the data. Without exclusion of the outliers, the averages of cost codes or jobs are skewed. **FIGURE 6–23** shows an outlier job and its effect before and after removal from the data set. It is critical to recognize that although every job has a story, not every job is an outlier.

Estimation must have feedback from both accounting and the job site to better predict the cost of the next project and to provide more reliable and predictable information to the company about whether it should pursue the next job. Averages and blanket pricing can mask the true issues. For example, the fixtures cost code may be an acceptable loss leader when it accounts for 20 percent or less of the labor on the job. However, the same cost code could be a killer when it accounts for 60 percent or more of the job. Consider that a cost code with $200,000 in labor on a $500,000 project

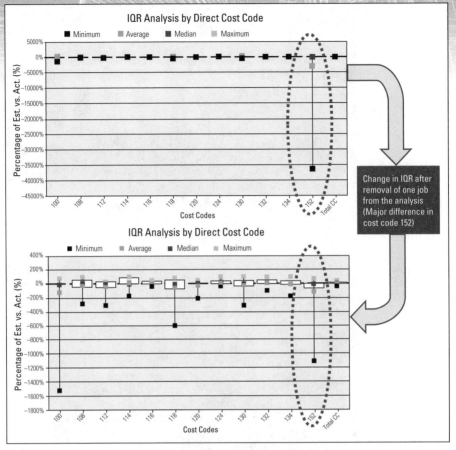

FIGURE 6–23 Impact of estimation analysis after removing one outlier job from the set.

has a considerably different impact than does the same cost code with $200,000 in labor on a $1,000,000 project. Jobs with a certain owner may be fine on a short schedule, but subject to huge overruns if the schedule expands. A crew can typically install a thousand feet of cable tray in a certain amount of time; however, drops and angles, especially those made in response to the physical reality of the job site and not necessarily evident on drawings, can significantly slow the rate of installation. So, using the production average from this job to predict the next leads to variation. Only when you analyze the job in context on the job site can you recognize the impacting factors and improve estimation. **FIGURE 6–24**

FIGURE 6–24 A complex run of pipe that was not foreseen in the estimate.

shows such an unpredictable change to the pipe run, which was caused by mismatch of the concrete slabs from one floor to the next.

Case Study

Understanding the similarities between jobs is the first step in breaking down the estimation and accounting data. **FIGURE 6–25** shows a sample category breakdown used by one electrical contractor. Once the categories are selected, the contractor can compare jobs on a cost code by cost code basis (**FIGURE 6–26**). The EAE program then compares data from accounting and estimation databases (**FIGURE 6–27**). The contractor can then statistically analyze the data. For example, **FIGURE 6–28** shows the difference between the entire job, and **FIGURE 6–29** shows the difference between the cost codes. As shown in these figures,

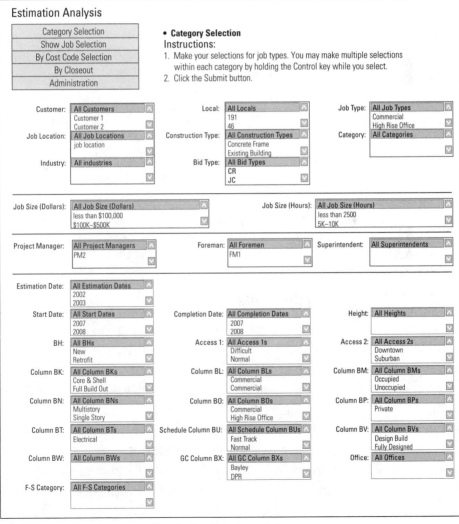

FIGURE 6–25 Categories set up to filter the list of jobs for analysis.

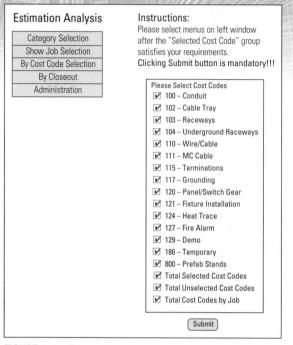

FIGURE 6–26 The analysis can also be limited to certain cost codes.

the overall job does not give a clear picture of the variation between estimates and actual until the jobs are broken down into cost codes.

FIGURE 6–30 shows the box plot of the cost code spread. The cost codes that have a wider spread are harder to predict, and you must deal with them cautiously. The cost codes with narrower spreads are much more predictable. Using another tool in the EAE, estimators can examine each cost code in terms of the validity of its estimate in comparison to the way the work is performed. In **FIGURE 6–31**, you can see examples of more and less predictable cost codes, as well as cost codes that are consistently overbid or underbid.

■ Using the Tools

Every contractor, project manager, and foreman intuitively knows that planning helps improve production; however, to know the magnitude of the impact, the processes must be quantified and measured. JPAC and SIS show the strong correlation of planning to productivity and therefore to profitability and identify how and when it is necessary to intercede. You can clearly see the correlation in **FIGURE 6–32**.

Together, SIS and JPAC form the backbone for monitoring and managing the company's labor management process by aiding in the operational management of daily activities, progress, and plans. With JPAC, managers can constantly monitor actual

Estimation Analysis

- Category Selection
- Show Cost Code Selection
- Hours Report by Jobs
- Estimation Deviation
- Estimation Deviation Comparison for Job
- Run Chart Comparison for Job
- Statistic IQR Analysis by Cost Code
- Administration
- Logout

Selected Job Set

- ☑ 1—job 1
- ☑ 2—job 2
- ☑ 3—job 3
- ☑ 4—job 4
- ☑ 5—job 5
- ☑ 6—job 6
- ☑ 7—job 7
- ☑ 8—job 8
- ☑ 9—job 9
- ☑ 10—job 10
- ☑ 11—job 11
- ☑ 13—job 13
- ☑ 17—job 17
- ☑ 22—job 22

Instructions:

1. This page shows the estimated and actual hours for the jobs you chose, broken down by cost code.
2. Use the navigation table to the left to view other analyses on your selected jobs and cost codes.

Number of Estimation Hours

	COST	CODE	NUMBER											
JOB NAME	011	012	016	017	021	024	026	027	028	030	037	Total SCC	Total SCC	TOTAL COST CODES BY JOB
1—job 1	18	607	160	0	567	0	1135	428	98	949	1116	5078	0	5078
2—job 2	—	2042	700	226	786	162	1126	2158	144	1074	2601	11019	0	11019
3—job 3	810	567	220	878	50	154	567	209	230	221	2943	6849	0	6849
4—job 4	—	873	120	1246	484	239	254	458	236	644	2994	7558	0	7558
5—job 5	24	12	180	—	98	—	63	327	42	181	3	930	0	930
6—job 6	50	490	80	439	31	97	437	350	166	603	1941	4684	0	4684
7—job 7	674	232	120	109	117	168	141	69	133	105	1239	3107	0	3107
8—job 8	583	202	120	132	169	166	193	197	137	162	1230	3291	0	3291
9—job 9	551	271	120	90	140	159	241	13	136	137	1369	3227	0	3227
10—job 10	576	330	120	94	83	203	245	18	141	151	1340	3301	0	3301
11—job 11	539	1457	120	2511	1488	757	2661	2721	811	1846	5412	20323	0	20323
13—job 13	—	68	120	174	20	4	25	202	44	383	244	1284	0	1284
17—job 17	965	1449	297	1542	295	311	598	589	416	747	5384	12593	0	12593
22—job 22	484	810	120	828	932	259	802	859	324	476	3144	9038	0	9038
72—job 72	300	128	120	93	919	40	1200	1686	267	782	726	6264	0	6264
Total by Cost Code	5574	9537	2717	8362	6179	2722	9688	10294	3325	8461	31685	98544	0	98544

FIGURE 6–27 Comparison of estimated and actual hours across cost codes and across jobs. *(Continues)*

Number of Actual Hours

JOB NAME	COST 011	CODE 012	NUMBER 016	017	021	024	026	027	028	030	037	Total SCC	Total SCC	TOTAL COST CODES BY JOB
1—job 1	48	371	71	8	430	365	506	864	34	761	1094	4552	0	4552
2—job 2	0	2496	49	72	1048	5	495	2140	133	3606	321	10364	0	10364
3—job 3	756	780	260	1489	123	103	448	46	44	420	4008	8573	0	8573
4—job 4	0	729	247	1840	227	332	93	469	74	768	3277	8054	0	8054
5—job 5	0	2	99	0	117	0	37	202	52	112	34	654	0	654
6—job 6	0	712	54	1031	53	352	355	433	88	201	2214	5490	0	5490
7—job 7	757	481	124	380	104	375	321	9	114	151	1879	4695	0	4695
8—job 8	478	242	43	235	167	214	223	79	72	188	1961	3902	0	3902
9—job 9	570	562	140	399	158	425	253	12	106	314	2273	5211	0	5211
10—job 10	422	422	116	356	83	216	266	62	129	145	1793	4008	0	4008
11—job 11	711	1037	146	3345	1375	735	2077	3639	327	2469	8121	23981	0	23981
13—job 13	0	103	83	212	38	1	2	44	29	178	403	1091	0	1091
17—job 17	558	1911	297	1753	248	529	310	646	19	935	5331	12534	0	12534
22—job 22	58	268	63	855	788	164	573	1294	160	645	2051	6917	0	6917
72—job 72	205	117	7	226	479	44	1595	1688	75	788	1561	6786	0	6786
Total by Cost Code	4562	10232	1896	12198	5435	3859	7552	11625	1455	11679	36318	106809	0	106809

FIGURE 6–27 (Continued)

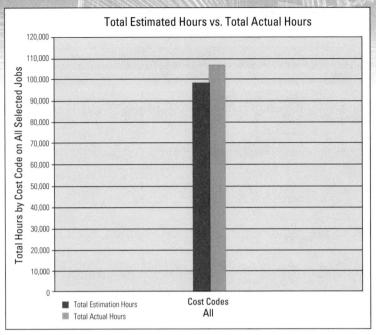

FIGURE 6–28 Comparison of total job estimated hours to total job actual hours.

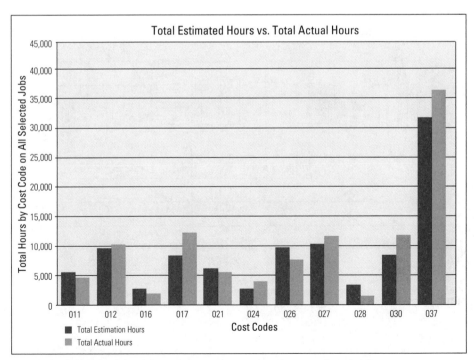

FIGURE 6–29 Comparison of estimated to actual hours across the cost codes on a job.

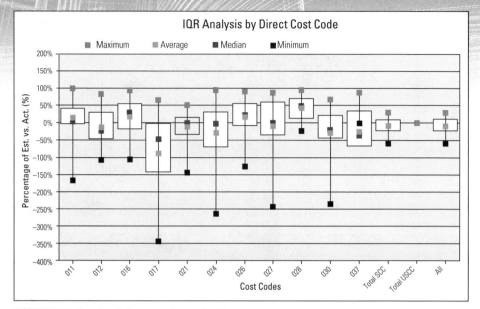

FIGURE 6–30 Box plot of the cost codes on the job.

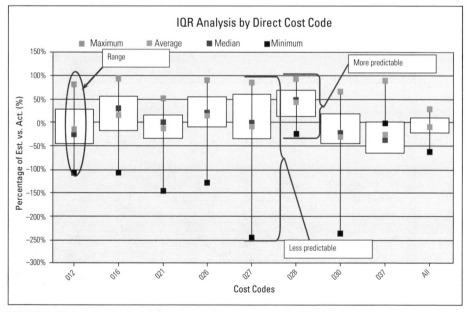

FIGURE 6–31 Box plot shows that some cost codes are more predictable than others.

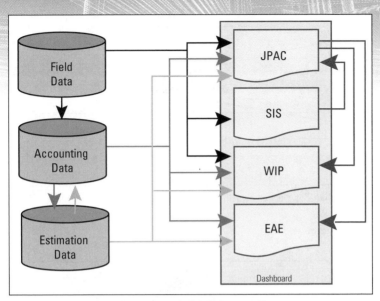

FIGURE 6–32 Correlation between JPAC, SIS, EAE, and WIP.

job productivity relative to planned base lines, and with SIS they can keep a watchful eye on factors that interfere with the labor's ability to work effectively and on schedule. At the job site level, JPAC and SIS help you track and quantify the impact of planning on productivity, and the impact of productivity on profitability.

The nucleus of job site productivity measurement is the run chart, which tracks the "how" and "what" of productivity while indicating how you should react to it. By using JPAC to indicate where and when productivity issues are occurring, and by scoring a SIS, the field supervisor can look for underlying root causes of productivity changes on the job. If the SIS cannot be planned and managed, the job loses productivity.

FIGURE 6–33 shows the direct relationship between the unplanned hours, as measured during the scoring of the SIS, and the job productivity, tracked with JPAC, over the same time frame. The two examples in **FIGURE 6–34** show three-week sections of the same project. When labor spends more hours on any activities other than those scheduled for the day, the job

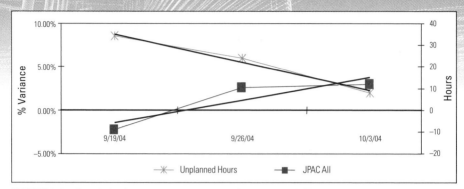

FIGURE 6–33 Correlation between unplanned hours (tracked with SIS) and productivity (tracked with JPAC).

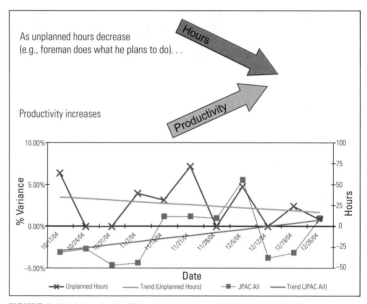

FIGURE 6–34 As unplanned hours decrease over time, productivity increases.

productivity declines. Conversely, when the job is worked as scheduled, in other words, when fewer hours are spent doing unscheduled or unanticipated work or no work, the overall productivity on the job increases.

By planning the progress, and then allowing the operator to indicate the ongoing progress against the plan at regular, frequent intervals, you can take action and make course corrections. With the direct evidence of the correlation between planning and productivity, and the resulting effect on profitability, there is no reason for you not to plan and execute.

Accounting measures often serve to muddy the water. Suppose that 1250 feet of conduit laid one day are removed the next and reconfigured and reinstalled to accommodate a new layout. If the labor reports the next day that they installed 600 feet of conduit, do you consider that 600 feet a reinstallation? Will the accounting measures show an installation of 1850 feet or only 600 because the original was uninstalled?

Typically, contractors mistakenly use accounting measurements of production, such as spent versus budgeted hours or dollars, as measurements of productivity, which is like driving using only the rearview mirror. By the time the data from operations in the field are scored, reported, and produced, weeks and sometimes months have passed. Many small responses and reactions have occurred that can no longer be differentiated. It is too late for the field to react and adjust.

However, the estimate and accounting data are not enough on their own. The visible differences between the initial estimates and the final profitability are primarily caused by different labor productivity in the field. In addition, electricians work differently on various cost codes. Measurements such as JPAC provide real-time feedback to estimation that accurately reflects how the construction is put in place. To see the entire picture and to be able to improve the accuracy of the estimation and profitability at the final accounting, the accounting data, the estimation data, and field productivity information must all be evaluated collectively and in context. The trends and patterns are every bit as important as the final numbers.

The quality of life for every American relies in part on the work and construction put in place by electrical contractors and other trades. By improving productivity by using Agile tools, you can help reduce the cost of living while increasing the quality of life. The tools by themselves cannot help you, but how you apply them can. This chapter introduces various time-tested and validated productivity tools. It is of the utmost importance that you think about the process of implementation and include your workforce in designing it. The impact of improved productivity on the bottom line can be much larger when company management uses their people's heads in addition to their hands.

Corporate Tools for Agile Construction

Developing a relationship with customers and vendors as an overall company strategy is a cornerstone of any contractor's operation. The company owners and executives should make decisions about customers and vendors with utmost care. And then, they should review these relationships periodically to see whether they can be improved.

Some tools of Agile contracting are strategic tools that the company executives select and put in place. Additionally, the company's executives must understand and design the internal reporting structure of each job's financial progress, commonly known as work in progress (WIP). When you use Agile procurement, you can focus on the value of the material versus the man-hours needed to manage that material. The man-hours lost to receiving, handling, returning, moving, and storing the material often are much more expensive than the potential savings from early purchases and payments.

■ Agile Procurement: Vendor Partnership

The Electrical Contracting Industry has come to a fork in the road of supply channel management. In their historical roles, distributors play the part of wholesale/retail suppliers of electrical components while hoping to make profits through speculation (currently on steel and copper), and contractors act as their own suppliers, buying in bulk and then paying far more in labor to manage their materials. Material purchasing by the general contractor or owner does little to help either the distributor's or contractor's costs and profits. By using an alternative model, Agile procurement, contractors and distributors can jointly manage the material flow in partnership.

Consider how much time is spent in the historical model when contractors and distributors negotiate a 1 percent or 2 percent price reduction. Ultimately, contractors and distributors are looking for the same thing: profits. Where do profits go? A couple of electricians waiting for a $2 bracket to arrive can accrue a net cost of hundreds or thousands of dollars. When a $15 red label (urgent) shipping tag is attached to a $20 package and the cost absorbed by the distributor, the entire profit and maybe more is lost. Both companies operate at a loss. This occurs on a daily basis throughout the industry.

Contractors and distributors have very different needs. By partnering, contractors and distributors form a close relationship and can identify each other's needs. For the partnership to work, the partners capitalize on each other's strengths to address their own needs. They understand that the profitability of the relationship goes far beyond the price of and gross profits made on materials, and they focus on reducing the inherent costs in the system. Each partner uses its expertise to meet the needs of the other so that distributors manage materials and distribution and contractors focus on productive installation. Creating a statement of work (SOW) is a good start to forming a partnership. (See **BOX 7–1** for an example.)

To build the elements of the partnership, distributors need to understand contractors—how they make money and where they earn their profits—as well as their own business model and where and how their profits are made. According to National Electrical Contractors Association (NECA) data, on average, a typical electrical contractor's revenues can be broken down as follows (see also **FIGURE 7–1**):

- Cost of labor: 42 percent
- Cost of materials: 34 percent
- Subcontracting: 4 percent
- Direct job expenses (overhead): 17 percent
- Profit: 3 percent

Within a small margin, the materials for a project are essentially fixed at a price set by the local market. For the contractor,

BOX 7–1 Partnership Statement of Work

1. Supplier will work with contractors to establish a standard set of terms and conditions for all matters involving the relationship between the contractor and the supplier.
2. Supplier agrees to cooperate with contractor to build a partnership that is founded on mutual trust and mutual concern for each partner's interests.
3. Supplier will work with contractor to ensure that the partnership results in a true "win-win" relationship on every job.
4. Supplier will work with contractor to ensure that each provides the other with unconditional support, as viewed from the contractor's client's perspective.
5. Supplier will work with contractor to define the terms and conditions under which contractor will use only a single vendor for commodities on each job site.
6. Supplier will work with contractor to develop and use a consistent and standard process to identify, monitor, and resolve issues.
7. Supplier will work with contractor to ensure that this strong partnership is leveraged as a sales and marketing channel for both organizations.
8. Supplier will work with contractor to provide a single point of contact for the management of this partnership, including follow-up and issue resolution.

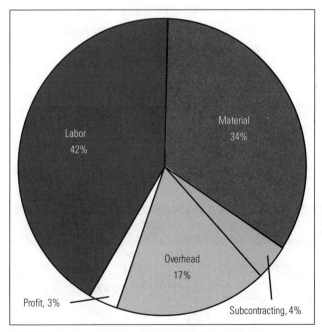

FIGURE 7–1 Average electrical contractor's revenue breakdown.

this makes labor the biggest variable. Labor is the factor with the largest impact on contractor profitability.

MCA's research shows that approximately 40 percent of the labor on a job goes to material handling in some form: receiving, unpacking, assembling, waiting, ordering, returning, fetching, locating; if contractors can decrease the 40 percent of the 42 percent total cost of labor, they can convert up to 17 percent of revenues from cost of labor to bottom-line profits. To achieve this same savings on material costs would require distributors to provide a 44 percent price cut—on everything.

In reality, you cannot recover 100 percent of the time spent on material handling. However, by using a vendor partnership, saving even a portion of that 40 percent translates directly and significantly to the bottom line. To achieve the savings, work together with the distributor to use its resources and exper- tise to address material management and distribution needs to facilitate the installation of the material. (See **TABLE 7–1** for cost savings comparison of material versus labor. This model is called Supply Chain Horizontal Integration [SCHI] or Vendor Partnership.)

When distributors provide services, it adds to their costs; contractors understand this and are willing to share the bur- den when it reduces their own overall costs. A recent survey for the Electrical Contracting Foundation (Named Electri 21) research project shows that more than 96 percent of contrac- tors are willing to pay for some distributor services (see Fig- ure 4–9 in Chapter 4). The savings attained through increased

TABLE 7–1 **Potential Savings for Contractors Applying the SCHI Model**		
Annual Sales	$10,000,000	
Material Purchase	$ 3,400,000	Potential savings @ 2% **$68,000**
Labor Cost	$ 4,200,000	Potential savings @ 40% **$1,680,000**

productivity substantially outweighs the direct cost of material or equipment.

For contractors to pay for services, distributors must accurately quantify the total cost of providing those services. Distributors can also leverage the resources and expertise of contractors to reduce the costs of providing such services. For example, in recent research for the National Association of Electrical Distributors (NAED), MCA found that every time the distributor processes a contractor's purchase order, it costs the distributor an average of $72, not including the actual material costs. That same purchase order also costs the contractor an average of $42, and research shows that the typical contractor processes 4000 purchase orders for every $10 million worth of sales.

The cost of providing services is hidden because the resources needed to provide them are in the fixed category. Fixed costs cannot be linearly divided across volume of material or volume of services. Compounding the service cost issue is the fact that many services are lumped in with material, further masking the distributor's cost of service. Quantifying resource allocation to individual services allows the most accurate pricing of distributor services.

For vendor partnerships to work, the biggest help a contractor can provide is communication and planning. By moving the customer point of entry forward as far as possible, distributors use the electrical contractor's intimate knowledge of the project to reduce their own costs. Frequent, early communication allows a distributor the flexibility to manage its inventory and processes in such a way as to be responsive instead of reactive. The distributor can identify and solve problems before they become emergencies.

In the partnership model, the contractor and distributor work together. For example, **FIGURE 7–2** shows a job box that contains the correct quantities of the correct materials delivered to a specific location on the job site immediately prior to when the contractor will begin the planned work. With proper planning and coordination, the distributor can provide this service,

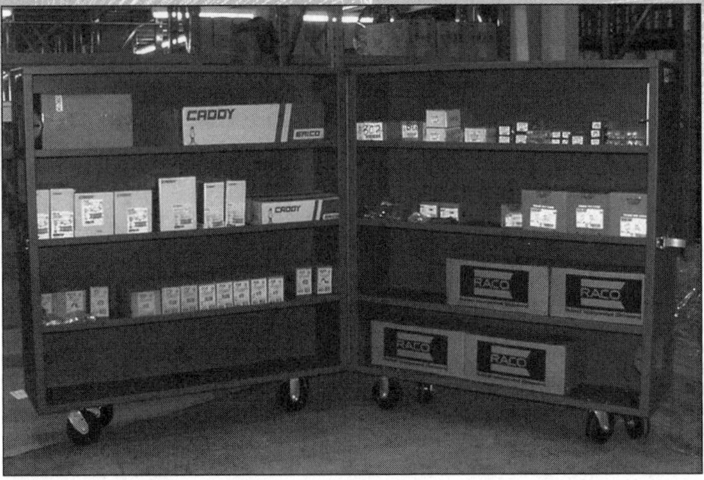

FIGURE 7–2 Job box stocked with correct type and quantity of material and delivered just before work begins.
Courtesy of Graybar.

freeing the contractor to focus on the installation. In a best practice application, the distributor and the contractor jointly develop a process of procurement that allows both parties to focus on their core competencies by sharing information and building on the strengths of the other.

■ Work in Progress

Construction is a business like any other business—it needs cash and profits to sustain itself and grow. In a profitable contracting business, the money coming in minus the money going out pays for overhead without sacrificing profit. To complete an electrical project, you need electricians (manpower), who in turn need material to install (material). To pay the electricians, buy the material, and pay for overhead, you need to have access to cash (money).

Construction contracting requires massive up-front investment prior to actual cash inflow. To estimate, win, and manage any project, you need to have at least 30 percent of the total value of the project available up front as cash or a line of credit (LOC). At any point in time, this readily available money supply must be able to carry 10 to 20 percent of the annual revenues of the company and must be available prior to any income from a project or even any billings on the project. Most subcontractors do not develop a positive cash flow on construction projects until the last 5 to 10 percent of the project, and some never do (see **FIGURE 7–3**).

Money is the common denominator in all construction jobs. To translate every activity into the common denominator of dollars, you must have a visible system that tracks the money in and out, like a cash register. The tools of Agile Construction™ focus on putting you in a position to run projects efficiently and manage profits correctly. In much the same manner that JPAC® and SIS™ provide true real-time situational awareness of the labor (manpower), productivity, and material availability (material), the work in progress (WIP) tool provides both high-level and detailed situational awareness of the financial position (money) of the overall company and each project. Creating an accurate WIP in Agile Construction is critical to your company's financial wealth and health.

WIP provides visibility of cash flow, profits, cash requirements, and overall financial performance on a job-by-job basis.

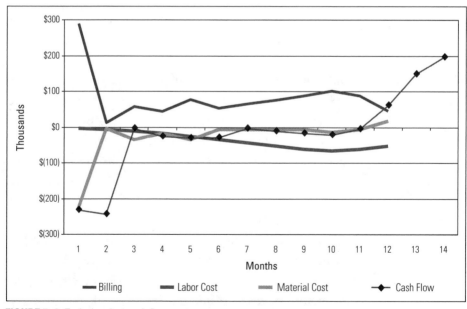

FIGURE 7–3 Typical project cash flow.

The primary goals of WIP are to identify job productivity and earned value, to ensure correct billing, and to ensure cash flows in a timely fashion. With accurate WIP information, you are better positioned to make intelligent and timely decisions about the financial performance of current and future jobs.

Accounting processes and accounting systems report the cash events as they have occurred; however, to balance and manage project cash flow project managers and company managers must operate ahead of the reporting. The dilemma you face is how best to balance the income, cash flow, billings, and expenditures. Early identification of potential cash problems for proactive (Agile) financial management requires a more detailed look at the interactions between the operations and the associated cash movement. A visible system that connects the operations to the sales, billings, and cash flow makes all of these more manageable for daily activities.

In an Agile company the role of accounting changes from one of reporting using a passive rearview mirror approach to being a proactive, forward-looking, and operational participant in the company's activities. Although accounting data are a critical component of the company's operation, accounting measurements in isolation do not provide the necessary context for you to fully evaluate and manage an ongoing construction project.

Because of the nature of the accounting principles such as GAAP (Generally Accepted Accounting Principles) used to manage company profitability, most measurements of job progress are in reality measurements of production or earned value. They omit productivity impact on the job site, or even worse, they assume that there is no productivity impact. This distinction directly affects the cash flow of both the project and the company as a whole.

It is a mistake to use accounting measurements of production to stand in as measurements for productivity. By the time the data from operations in the field have been scored, reported, and produced, weeks or months have passed. This accounting approach significantly reduces your agility in the field and does not allow you to respond immediately to special causes occurring on the project.

Another prevalent mistake in contracting is confusing sales and billings. The fact of the matter is that sales have little to do with billings. A sale occurs when goods and services are exchanged for an agreed price. In contrast, billings are the amount that you invoice a customer for work completed. Confusing the two could cost you tens of thousands of dollars in revenues and taxes and seriously restrict your ability to respond to the needs of projects. However, when percent completion is measured as an integral part of job productivity tracking, you can determine and use true job progress to address the operational needs and issues of the project as they occur.

When you have access to accurate and timely information on job progress from the field in conjunction with accounting data, you can manage the project more efficiently and manage the entire company more profitably. By expanding the WIP to reflect the job site productivity, you can better manage cash flow in response to the true needs of the company because without adequate cash flow, your company cannot survive.

How to Create a WIP

The WIP comprises three fundamental elements: sales, billings, and the scope of work completed. The typical detail categories of a basic WIP are as follows (see also **FIGURE 7–4**):

- Contract values (base amount plus approved changes)
- Contract cost estimates (base amount plus approved changes)
- Original estimated profit margin (with and without approved changes)
- Job cost to date
- Value of completed construction
- Actual billings
- Over/underbilling
- Projected profit margin

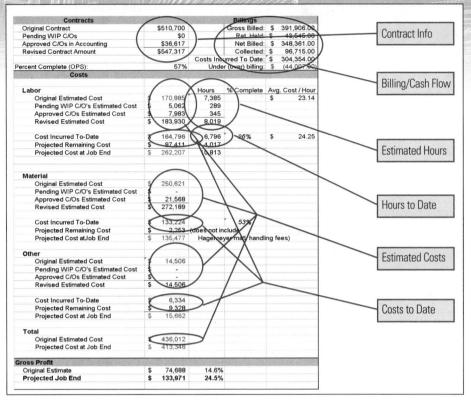

FIGURE 7–4 Components of a typical WIP report.

The WIP calculation relies on a combination of hard numbers (actual job costs, actual billing amounts, and revised contract values) as well as the project manager's reasoned evaluation of the following:

- Construction put in place (value of the scope of work completed)
- Projected cost to complete the remaining work
- Value of pending changes and extra work

At any point in the project, the WIP reports the earned value based on the higher of observed percentage complete or cost-to-cost completion (described later in this chapter). With this maximum, you can recognize productivity gains without losing sight of large up-front material purchases. The WIP report should also show actual billings in relation to this earned value calculation, to allow for billing not only cost but also profit associated with improved productivity.

One of the most misunderstood concepts in the construction industry is the difference between profitability and cash flow. Profitability is the difference between the contract price and the costs incurred to complete the job. The cash flow is determined by comparing the amount received from the customer to the actual project costs paid to date. The WIP report uses two fundamental and critical measures to help monitor and manage cash flow on the project. First, it identifies the amount billed for the scope of work that has been delivered and, second, it identifies the money collected from the customer in the following forms:

- Project billings to date (invoice totals)
- Cash collected to date (payments received against these invoices)

When costs to date exceed the amount collected, the WIP shows a negative number (cash short). When received cash exceeds the paid costs, the WIP shows a positive number (cash over).

Work in progress measures must take into account labor productivity on the job site and the actual flow of work. Managing jobs based on costs results in unpredictable outcomes. Often, you do not know until the end of the job whether you will earn the expected profits. Progress reporting that recognizes variations in labor productivity changes the way you look at jobs, both operationally and financially.

The WIP report also identifies your billing status in terms of over/underbillings. Overbilling occurs when you issue billings for more than the sales made to date. Underbilling occurs when billings are less than the sales to date. In the WIP, these amounts are separate so that you can evaluate the total overbilled and total underbilled statuses, as opposed to monitoring only your net over/underbilled status. This distinction is critical and overlooked by many accounting reports. The fact that one job is overbilled does not justify having another job underbilled by the same amount.

You can expand the basic WIP report to include other useful management tools to create a visible snapshot of the project, department, and company financial health and associated risk areas. (See **FIGURE 7–5** for a sample WIP report.) You can design a more detailed WIP report to help CFOs, accountants, and owners accurately predict future cash flows and potential write downs (or ups) using data that are available early in the project life cycle. This early prediction increases your responsiveness and agility, while preserving or enhancing profitability. Both project and company managers can refine profit and cash flow projections based on actual job productivity experience while taking into consideration estimated, actual, and committed costs.

The importance of WIP and its accuracy becomes even clearer when the situation on a job site is not reported correctly. The actual data in the accounting system may be correct but may not be a true reflection of the project. For example, project managers are often responsible for billing on a project. Suppose the project manager (PM) wants to save some profits as a buffer to cover any last-minute hiccups or embarrassments at the end of the job. On a $1 million job, the project manager may report 10 percent less on the earned profits. Assuming that the job will make 15 percent at any given time, the underreporting is 1½ percent, or $150,000 × 0.1 = $15,000. Because of the underreporting, this amount is not billed and collected by the contractor until the end of the project. The contractor must replace this cash flow either from savings or by borrowing. If the contractor has to borrow money, the interest on the loan reduces overall job profits. This underreporting is equivalent to carrying a full-time electrician at $30 per hour for 500 hours without an income stream.

Another situation arises when the jobs are measured only against an initial estimate by looking at cost to complete. For reasons including complexity, access, timing, and workload, a project manager may not track current costs by updating the accounting system. At one sample company, job budgets were updated in the accounting system only after 90 percent

Basic Work in Progress (WIP)

August 8, 2007

Jobs in Progress

Job Number	Project Name	Original Contract Value	Approved Changes	Revised Contract Value	Percent Complete	Construction Put in Place	Actual Billing	Over / (Under) Billing	Est. Cost to Complete	Orig. Profit Estimate	Projected Profit	Original Est. Cost	Est. Cost of Changes	Job Cost to Date
001-2007	Downhome Grocery	$ 86,000	$ 5,000	$ 91,000	80.0%	$ 72,822	$ 69,500	$ (3,322)	$ 14,500	9.0%	12.1%	$ 78,229	$ 3,650	$ 65,523
002-2007	Suburban Auto Center	$ 112,000	$ 12,670	$ 124,670	32.7%	$ 40,706	$ 55,000	$ 14,294	$ 85,000	17.6%	6.2%	$ 92,337	$ 95,500	$ 31,945
010-2007	At Home Apartments	$ 32,991	$ 530	$ 33,521	80.9%	$ 27,133	$ 3,299	$ (23,834)	$ 5,400	21.5%	21.1%	$ 25,888	$ 110	$ 21,044
012-2007	Super Speed Deliveries	$ 2,200	$ —	$ 2,200	72.1%	$ 1,586	$ —	$ (1,586)	$ 465	41.4%	36.6%	$ 1,290	$ —	$ 930
014-2007	THY Manufacturing, Inc.	$ 639,192	$ 92,035	$ 731,147	59.8%	$ 437,510	$ 225,450	$ (212,060)	$ 421,000	5.9%	-12.5%	$ 601,218	$ 70,377	$ 401,875
	Company Totals	$ 872,303	$ 110,235	$ 982,538	59.3%	$ 579,758	$ 353,249	$ (226,509)	$ 526,365	8.4%	-6.6%	$ 798,962	$ 79,637	$ 521,317

Closed Projects

Job Number	Project Name	Original Contract Value	Approved Changes	Revised Contract Value	Percent Complete	Construction Put in Place	Actual Billing	Over / (Under) Billing	Est. Cost to Complete	Orig. Profit Estimate	Projected Profit	Original Est. Cost	Est. Cost of Changes	Job Cost to Date
067-2006	THY Manufacturing Ph1	$ 349,000	$ 128,111	$ 477,111	100.0%	$ 477,336	$ 477,111	$ (225)	$ —	12.9%	15.4%	$ 303,979	$ 99,472	$ 403,641
078-2006	City Hall—offices	$ 129,000	$ 41,321	$ 170,321	97.2%	$ 165,618	$ 170,321	$ 4,703	$ —	20.8%	24.8%	$ 102,222	$ 29,412	$ 127,999
	Company Totals	$ 478,000	$ 169,432	$ 647,432	99.4%	$ 642,953	$ 647,432	$ 4,479	$ —	15.0%	17.9%	$ 406,201	$ 128,884	$ 531,640

FIGURE 7–5 A sample WIP report

Source: "WIP Online" A MyWEM product by MCA Soft, Inc.

of the estimated costs of the project had been applied. In other words, only when the project manager was in danger of showing a loss on the books would he update the initial figures to represent the current estimated costs and profits on the project (**FIGURE 7–6**).

To simplify project tracking and comply with reporting requirements, many contractors reduce jobs and WIP reports to a strictly financial picture. Although using only financial measures allows simpler comparison between projects, it also allows net reporting, which often masks the job-specific events that ultimately drive the company's cash position. Although production data are important for managers responsible for the financial health of the company, production data without accompanying productivity measures do little to help you truly improve project performance.

There are different methods of reporting progress. JPAC reporting requires a physically observed completion to correctly evaluate productivity; other methodologies for recognizing completion may be seen in financial data and billing numbers. An understanding of each of these methodologies, as well as

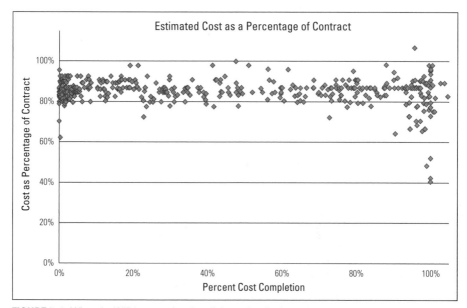

FIGURE 7–6 When the WIP is not updated until the project is almost complete.

the differences between them and how the differences affect the financial position, is critical to understanding your WIP.

Productivity-Based WIP Reporting

When you use WIP in conjunction with JPAC, the most powerful management information becomes available. On a regular and ongoing basis, JPAC provides a projection of labor hours required to complete the contract scope obligation at the currently known level of labor productivity. You can use this amount to refine end-of-job profitability and future cash flow projections constantly and accurately.

Contractors use three methods to determine completion of a project in terms of revenue recognition:

1. **Cost-to-cost based on the percentage of incurred cost.** This is the most commonly used method. Cost-to-cost is based on an assumption that the initial estimate is accurate or revised promptly when changes occur, and that the labor productivity does not vary from the budgeted units. The greatest advantage is that it requires no input from the field. The greatest disadvantage is that there is no indication of the completion point until the end of the job, and the cost can exceed 100 percent of estimated cost, without bounds.

2. **Unit-of-work performance measure.** This is another fairly common practice. The unit-of-work method requires careful monitoring and tracking of all material and labor applied in great detail, often using hundreds of cost codes. The greatest advantage is that it provides feedback to estimation in the manner that most closely monitors material. Again, there is no indication of the completion point until the end of the job, and the units can exceed 100 percent of estimated units, without bounds.

3. **Effort-expended based on physical completion through observation.** The effort expended method is rapidly gaining popularity among contractors. This method is based on the concept that the contract terms require 100 percent completion of the defined scope—not use of 100 percent

of the budgeted cost or planned hours. The greatest advantage is that this is the only way to gain early detection and estimation of the completion point and detect variations in productivity, not just production rates. The greatest disadvantage is that this requires that the project team understand the scope of the project.

JPAC-based WIP reporting uses the third method, which enables you to bill based on observed percentage complete. This method allows you a higher cash flow.

■ Customer Positioning and Control

Visibility and measurement are the main reasons Agile methods affect operational efficiencies and overall profitability. Operational and accounting measurements have to work hand in hand to make the results of the agility visible and meaningful.

It is well known that some projects contribute more to a company's profitability than others do. The activities of a job and how they are performed and integrated are what separates the "good" from the "bad." Some types of work or divisions of the company are inherently more efficient and profitable than others are. In the past, companies have relied solely on experience to filter the results. However, contractors who measure and understand their cost drivers can better manage the impact of those drivers and improve their productivity by a verifiable 20 to 30 percent.

The Customer Positioning and Control model (CPAC®) identifies the demands that your customers or projects place on resources relative to profitability and revenue. For example, **FIGURE 7–7** shows examples of various types of work and customer impact on the contractor's costs. The horizontal axis defines dollars (revenue or profits earned) per hour. The vertical axis shows revenue or profits over the cost incurred. Customers or projects in the upper right quadrant are the most profitable. Projects in quadrants II and III are still good, but can be improved through a more effective use of resources. Customers or projects that fall in quadrant IV (the lower left) are not profitable and must be dealt with strategically.

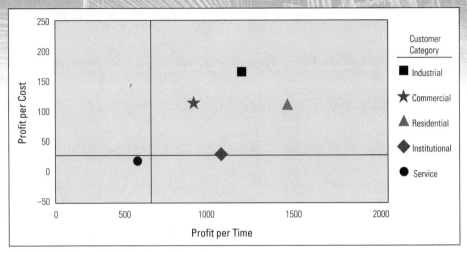

FIGURE 7–7 Customer Positioning and Control.

With CPAC, areas of strength and weakness become visible. For example, in an estimating department with three estimators, how much effort goes toward writing new work, how much toward reestimating work that is already in-house, and how much to working with project managers and field personnel to understand what was included in the pricing model on a particular project? As you implement plans to address weak areas that produce insufficient profits or significant costs, CPAC monitors the effects of these changes over time and will let you know if your changes are helping the process to improve.

Strategy for Agile

Agility does not end with day-to-day operations. Agile electrical contractors require Agile strategies to help their companies maneuver through good and bad times. To build an Agile strategy and secure your future, you must understand the construction market and its shifts from one category to another over time. For example, the current shift from industrial type of work to commercial-residential will require different types of training and strategies for market dominance than have been used in the last two decades.

Market Realities

Why Agile? The need for agility increases in the face of a changing economy. The perception of changing markets is real, as is the growth of residential-commercial expansion. The United States economy has shown a 3 to 4 percent increase in gross domestic product (GDP) per year on average over the last 20 years (**FIGURE III–1**). Recent growth has primarily occurred in the service and nonmanufacturing segments. The construction industry, which is driven by population and economic forces, has no choice but to follow this trend.

Since the early 20th century, a market's size and its characteristics, that is, its aggregation and segments, have been primary indicators of its health. Since the early 1960s, market measurements in the construction industry show a very clear

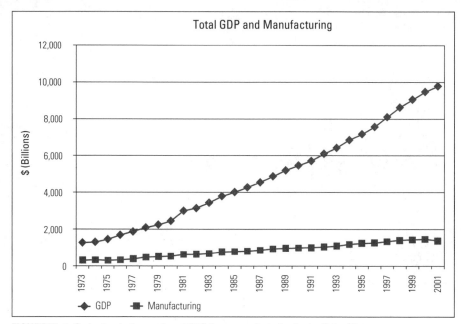

FIGURE III–1 Reduction in the portion of GDP from manufacturing in the United States.

shift from industrial to commercial-residential. Understanding the characteristics and changes in local as well as national markets is critical to an organization's ability to perform profitably and productively. Trends in construction market size—the dollars spent on construction (**FIGURE III–2**)—show a transformation in the 1960s when the construction market shifted from industrial construction to commercial-residential construction. More than 50 percent of the dollars spent in the construction market in 1955 were spent on industrial construction as compared to 28 percent spent on industrial construction in 2005.

Mirroring that trend, in the late 1990s the electrical construction market made its own shift from more than 50 percent industrial work to more than 50 percent commercial and residential work (**FIGURE III–3**). Much of the shift has been a result of the rapid growth in the commercial-residential markets. Over the next 20 years, the expansion of the market will continue

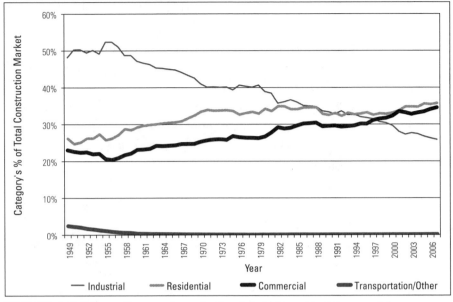

FIGURE III–2 Shift in overall construction market from industrial to residential-commercial.

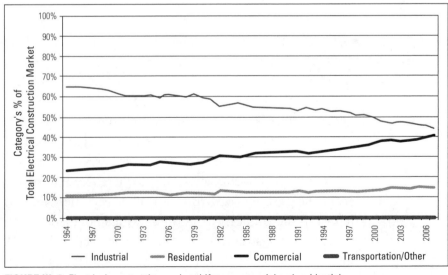

FIGURE III–3 Electrical construction market shift to commercial and residential.

to be in the commercial-residential area, which is driven by customer demands for growth: U.S. demographic trends predict a doubling of current floor space because the U.S. population is expected to increase by another 20 to 25 percent.

The landscape of the national construction and electrical construction markets follows the nation's socioeconomic growth. The risks and opportunities associated with construction increase each year as the work available in the marketplace shifts. The continuing shift from an industrial market to a commercial-residential market poses a challenge to many contractors. The cost of labor and its uncertainty are primarily driven by management practices, most prominently job site management and the consistent application of management processes.

A service-based national economy forces the majority of construction to be in commercial-residential sectors, which requires stronger production and managerial skills than have been used for the industrial type of projects. Technical skill is no longer the defining requirement of the industry. Agile companies must rethink their training programs and provide management skills training for foremen and supervisors in the commercial and residential markets.

Many large cities, such as New York, Chicago, and Los Angeles, are the sites of service-based and the softer economies of financial services, insurance, corporate headquarters, tourism, entertainment, software manufacturing, and medical and biotech research, among other enterprises. The Sunbelt cities, such as Phoenix and Dallas, where the majority of economic growth is occurring, are all newer cities and also represent the youngest cities, those with a population with the lowest median age. Among all the cities studied by MCA Inc., Detroit alone still recognizes manufacturing as its primary economy.

The large city markets represent the trend in expansion of commercial and residential work and a decline in industrial, not only within the city, but also in the surrounding suburban areas. However, nationally, the work available in large cities is declining as an entirety specifically in the commercial and industrial markets (**FIGURE III–4**), even as growth occurs on the outskirts and outside the cities.

The market shift is also the driving force behind the profitability of contractors because of the nature of the new markets and the skills required by different types of work. This shift is a concern for electrical contractors because it directly affects the dollars available in the economy for electrical work. The characteristics of the available construction work determine the amount and profitability of the associated electrical work. Nationally, for each dollar spent on industrial construction, on average 13 cents is for electrical work. For each dollar spent on commercial construction, 8 cents is for electrical; only about 3 cents per dollar spent on residential construction is available for the electrical portion of the job. These numbers vary greatly by location and type of work.

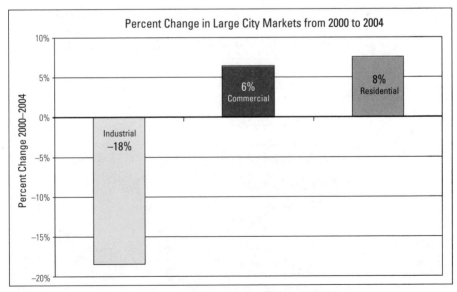

FIGURE III–4 Shift in the market in 25 large U.S. cities from 2000 to 2004.

Reliable information about the available work as well as how the electrical contractor performs in that market is essential to agility.

An Agile approach is required to remain competitive in the face of shifting markets. By recognizing the growth in and differences between markets and by differentiating between various segments of the electrical market, you can strategically approach the up-and-coming markets rather than be forced into a reactive position. This strategic response includes implementing new training, labor preparation, and integration to accommodate the faster economic cycles that are characteristic of the current service-oriented economy

You can control your target markets only if you are profitable. As technical skill becomes more widespread, you can be profitable only if you are a low-cost provider. Low cost is not the same as *cheap*, however; low-cost providers of construction services can provide high-quality work at a lower cost through higher system productivity and increased agility.

To respond to the new work environments, you must rethink old approaches and plan for the following circumstances:

- Appropriate utilization of lower ratios of specialized electricians
- Management of the work:
  - Material management and handling
  - People management
  - Time management
- Training and education of the workforce on productivity

In the commoditized commercial-residential market, you must become Agile by using appropriate data for the following processes:

- Estimation accuracy
- Productivity
- Trend monitoring

- Production data analysis
- Market impact of work type and location studies

Stronger, more standardized technical training can actually work against contractors who expect their electricians to improve productivity on their own. No matter how well trained in technical skills, capable, and knowledgeable electricians are, they cannot immediately stand in for field management. Yet often, because of their technical skill, electricians are put in charge of a large portion of project planning. In reality, their high level of training often leads to the "throw it over the wall" mindset of the traditional operating model, where each department assumes that the next knows what to do with information and passes it on in a very unstructured process (**FIGURE III–5**).

You can see a substantial productivity increase when you focus on production skills and use a supervisory workforce who are aggressively trained in proven managerial practices. Additional agility comes when you emphasize improved communication between electricians, foremen, superintendents, and project managers throughout the project and all the way to project postmortem meetings, which should include representatives from all departments involved with the job.

New markets require an Agile response in terms of management, training, and operational models. Those contractors flexible enough to respond to the changing environment are the

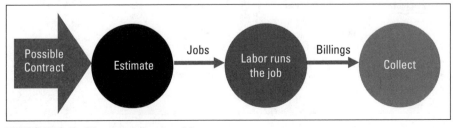

FIGURE III–5 Traditional operational model.

ones who can focus on productivity, job site needs, competitiveness, and profitability. Agile contractors use the right data and the right information to apply sound management principles.

■ How to Build an Agile Company: Strategic Planning

To build an Agile company, start by planning and identifying the sources of data you need for quick and correct responses to job site needs. By planning for agility, you effectively design the path that the company will pursue. Following are the core elements of strategic planning. Each has a different effect in different markets, so you must carefully investigate and localize your response to the following factors to address how to improve productivity and increase agility in the strategic plan (see also **FIGURE III–6**):

* Environment (markets)
* People (skills)

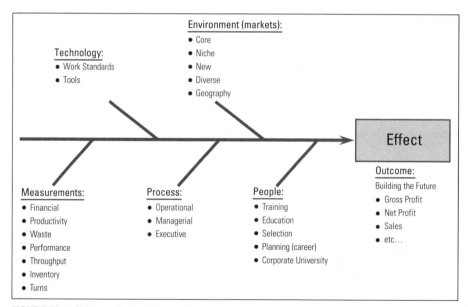

FIGURE III–6 Fishbone diagram of a strategic plan.

- Process (management)
- Measurements
- Technology (tools)

Be sure to use complete and reliable data sources to make successful decisions according to local market conditions. Other industries have found that maintaining former levels of market penetration in a specialized area while the market grows and expands has the inevitable effect of lost market share. With the loss in market share comes a corresponding loss in competitiveness, profitability, and employment.

Agile strategic planning requires you to use information that correctly and consistently recognizes the trends in markets. Your methodology must allow you to pursue and find solutions for the root causes of the issues addressed, because unless the right data are segregated correctly, market shifts and differences remain invisible. The lack of visibility is exaggerated in large companies where multiple types of work or multiple projects occur simultaneously. By recognizing and taking advantage of the significant differences in markets, you can plan and operate successfully in these markets.

When you apply the techniques of Agile Construction™, the accounting department can play a major role in connecting and interpreting the following three data sources for the company (see Figure 6–32):

- Estimation
- Project operation (project management and firsthand field data)
- Accounting

By correctly recognizing productivity and special and common causes, you can mine accounting data to improve the estimating hit ratio. Estimating needs the segregated feedback from both accounting and the field to improve labor rate and cost estimates. By measuring the project using JPAC®, you can help the accounting department improve job predictability and the company's cash flow position.

Responsiveness to the ever-changing environment of the construction job site is the key to profitability. To manage profits, the costs must be visible. By recognizing costs, you can become much more Agile in response to the job site's shifting needs.

The Supporting Structure for Agile Companies

Agility in a company is not a one-time event. To benefit from the overall impact of the Agile approach, the entire company's infrastructure and beliefs have to support Agile Construction™ and become responsive to Agile approaches. This chapter introduces the beliefs, requirements, and underlying processes that you can use to achieve a sustainable Agile Construction operation.

Company Infrastructure

To be Agile is to be responsive throughout the entire system. Every activity must purposefully and productively drive value for the customer. The system must be dynamic and responsive, continually sending signals for evaluation of its processes so that management can perpetually reduce waste. Agile companies do not just happen; they are designed.

Industries that have already improved their productivity embrace fundamental organizational principles, which are explained later in this chapter. Fortunately, these principles are universal and apply across all industries. The importance of these principles is underscored by the fact that a company cannot be Agile unless the entire company embraces the Agile approach and puts into place the supporting structure. To build the structure necessary to support Agile operations in electrical contracting, you must understand and apply the key organizational principles, which will enable your company to improve its productivity and reduce its internal costs. These principles fall into five major categories:

- System design
- Organizational learning

- Process models (visibility of systems and processes)
- Team technology
- Methods, algorithms, and tools (technologies)

System Design: Simplicity and Function

The underlying philosophy of design in an Agile organization is to focus on synthesis—to design a system that allows the components, the departments, and the functions in the company to integrate smoothly.

The inherent differences in the structure, style, and function of field and office in electrical contracting often results in suboptimization in direct violation of this principle. Designing an operation that concentrates on improving one area based on the need of just one department rather than of the entire system results in suboptimization and violates the system design principles.

For example, based on a survey of foremen from more than two thousand companies across the United States, MCA identified the 10 most costly causes of nonproductive time, as listed in **BOX 8–1**. However, the SIS™ results, as mentioned in Chapter 6, tell a different story (see Figure 6–12). The reason for this discrepancy is the fact that the labor will report the instantaneous issues impacting his output and not the root cause, which very often is different than the effect. For example, if the labor can not perform the scheduled activity due to the lack of

---

BOX 8–1 The 10 Most Costly Causes of Nonproductive "Wait Time"

1. Waiting for material—at warehouse or offsite
2. Waiting for tools and equipment
3. Waiting for equipment breakdowns to be fixed
4. Rework as a result of design, prefabrication, or field errors
5. Interfacing with other crews
6. Overcrowded work areas
7. Workplace changes
8. Waiting on permits
9. Waiting for instructions
10. Other delays, the most common of which is waiting for scaffolding to be put up or taken down

access to an area and has to improvise and do something else with the time available, he may run out of material. He will report material shortage as the reason for reduced productivity and not the lack of access. This may cause the office and project management to work to reduce material and tool problems, where they should have focused on lack of access.

System design principles rely on reduction of valueless variance, time, and activities (see **FIGURE 8–1**). Valueless variance is the inconsistency introduced into the system by a suboptimized process flow. For a contractor, valueless variance increases operating costs by adding the cost of punch lists that are unnecessary for well-planned jobs. For example, jobs where more time was spent on planning and prefabrication show a lower punch list and higher profits (see **FIGURE 8–2**).

Valueless activities are activities introduced into the system that are unnatural to the process flow, that increase transactions without providing additional value to the final product or services. For example, material handling on the job site by the foreman instead of by lower-skilled electricians is a valueless activity.

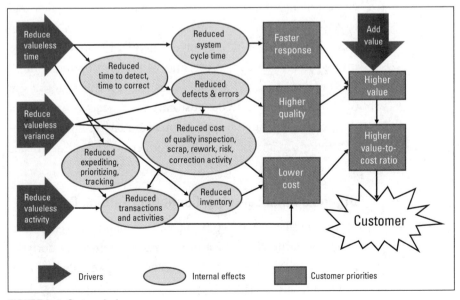

FIGURE 8–1 System design.

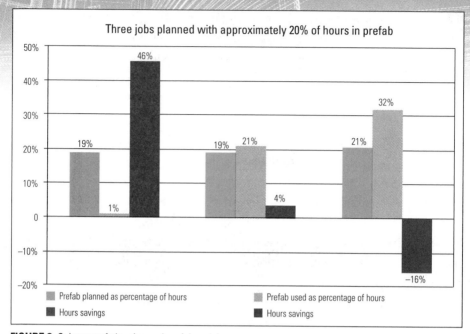

FIGURE 8–2 Impact of planning and prefab on labor usage.

By improving valueless time, variation, and activities, the products or services you provide will have lower cost, higher quality, and faster turnaround. Simultaneously, fewer defects and errors result in less rework, fewer corrective activities, and fewer transactions. Figure 8–1 illustrates the impact of reduction of the three valueless impediments of system design as improvements in time, cost, and value from the customer's perspective. Agile contractors must design the system from the job's and therefore the customer's perspective. Only from this perspective can the application of system design principles effectively streamline the value production and reduce chaos throughout the entire job.

Organizational Learning: Continual Learning Culture

Just as job sites are in a constant state of change, so is the company. Development of a learning culture is a major underlying principle in an Agile company because you can only maintain agility through continuous learning. A company cannot remain Agile if it relies on old models.

Learning can be accidental or planned. The organization can learn from its mistakes as well as from its improvements. By applying the results of learning to new projects, you can anticipate and plan appropriate responses, thereby reducing costs and increasing profits.

In today's environment of quickly changing markets, learning and adaptation are as critical as daily operations and income. A contractor without continuous learning and continuous improvement processes designed into operational activities cannot achieve or maintain a lead position in the field.

Different functions of the company face different risks during the life cycle of a project. At the project level, information must be gathered from the field and fed through the company in a continuous cycle, up through management, into accounting, and back through estimation to the pursuit of the next project.

In an Agile Construction company, you must develop the learning cycles on several levels, including the primary or cost code level, secondary or project level, and tertiary or company level, for the express purpose of completing a construction project:

- *Primary organizational learning:* Finding solutions for immediate individual issues
- *Secondary organizational learning:* Improving procedures and methods
- *Tertiary organizational learning:* Changing processes, principles, and/or operational models

An example of observed variation between the measured productivity and budgeted hours reported by timesheets through the accounting system will illustrate the three levels of learning.

Primary learning focuses on addressing immediate issues using conflict resolution methods. In this example, the weekly JPAC® charting identifies the instant job issues. At the primary level, the project manager and general foreman (GF) try to resolve the issue instantaneously as it relates to the job operations.

If the issue occurs more than once and can be tracked in SIS, you can use secondary learning to improve the conditions causing the issue, for instance, if the same distributor constantly misses their delivery time and date, then a meeting with the distribution's top management is required to ask for better service for all the jobs.

Tertiary learning occurs at the company level when the results from secondary learning procedural improvements indicate an entire process must be redesigned. If the same issues such as bad payment history from the same general contractor (GC) repeatedly happen in all the jobs dealing with that contractor, then the company may decide not to work with the GC or add penalties and extra cost of carrying the account receivables to their total project price. By comparing the SIS and JPAC results on all jobs and their impact on financial performance and using the accounting data, the company owners can make fundamental changes to improve overall processes. If a distributor, for example, affects performance positively or negatively on all jobs, management must review the company's relationship with the distributor to see whether it can be improved.

Additionally, you must spend a substantial amount of time educating and reeducating your whole organization on Agile concepts. Until the whole organization understands the fundamentals of Agility, you cannot benefit from the techniques. Do not fall short on education or believe a one-time training session will align everyone in the organization. Agility is a lifelong journey of continuous learning.

Process Models: Visibility of Systems and Processes

With visible process models in Agile construction, you can understand the workflow, job requirements, and interactions between field labor and departments as they currently exist within the company. In addition to measuring quality and value, with visible systems you can measure and understand costs so that you can more effectively manage operational efficiencies and overall profitability. In an Agile system, the process models must make the value delivered to the customer visible throughout the system. By implementing the models, you can examine the system for logic, waste, and valueless activities.

Electrical contractors provide low-cost, high-quality, fast construction projects; these must be the criteria on which the process model is evaluated. As the value to the customer from each stage of production becomes visible within the system, the quality of workmanship also becomes visible and can be translated into perceived customer value. According to W. E. Deming and Ron Moen, leaders in quality improvement, quality is nothing less than "translating needs of the customer into measurable characteristics."

Team Technology: Dimensions of Information Flow Control and Communications

The increasing complexities of work environments and technical know-how have forced many contractors to divide work by specialty area. Specialization, however, results in reduced information flow within and between areas. In addition, any time information is exchanged between departments, a gap exists, allowing an opportunity for possible misinformation or missing information to creep in. This gap at the point of discontinuity between processes also forces an unwanted disturbance in the quality of work performed.

For example, the workflow in the estimating department is very different from the workflow in the accounting department. The estimator may not need specific contract requirements, such as taxation requirements or other governmental specifications, to estimate the job order, yet the accounting department cannot complete the project billing without those vital pieces of information. Because estimators do not consider this information essential to their work, they may overlook or omit it, which then requires the accounting department to perform unwanted extra steps of recalculating the cost of project and schedules of payments.

In another example, a project manager who does not coordinate material needs with the field for receiving and installation and with the office for purchasing and accounts payable can introduce significant rework and lost productivity in both areas: in the field by causing the labor not to be prepared to receive or install the material when it is delivered, and in the office by forcing personnel to spend hours trying to reconcile purchase orders, invoices, and billings.

On the other hand, when the field foreman knows of upcoming changes in the schedule that are the result of the activities of other trades on the job site, he can use this advance knowledge to better distribute crews as needed among multiple job sites.

The throughput of a company shows the information channel, and the bandwidth of the throughput is a measure of how much information is shared between departments. Figure II–1 in the Part II introduction illustrates these concepts for different activities in an electrical contracting job. Activities that occur outside the bandwidth may not be essential to the completion of the activity but have developed out of necessity to meet the needs of a particular department. Bandwidth widens when there is more interaction between departments and that interaction focuses on the common goal of service to the customer. More information is carried through and shared, such as essential contract information, helping to reduce waste and rework. Constraints and bottlenecks limit the bandwidth and restrict the flow of information.

Consider a small electrical contracting company in which the owner can do everything himself. He has complete knowledge of all operations and does not need to explain anything to anyone. However, as his sales volume increases, he needs to hire people: a warehouse manager, estimator, project manager, and so forth. Information no longer flows as smoothly as before. Profits per job are reduced. With increased help, he earns less money on each contract dollar sold. To increase profits, the company needs to regain the complete knowledge that the owner had in the beginning.

Department workflow and structure strongly affect the leaning of the organization. By using team technology and cross-functional teams, the contractor can optimize his workflow and smoothly transition between departments with full information intact. To increase the bandwidth of information flow and cause a resulting increase in capability and capacity, the cross-functional team must complete the following tasks:

- Understand the contractor's core competencies
- Identify the specialties needed to deliver the core competencies
- Understand the workflow requirements of each department
- Identify the workflow and information-flow bandwidth
- Increase the capability of the entire system

Methods, Algorithms, and Tools (Technologies)

When a company aspires to quick results and neglects to apply strategic thinking, it tends to look to tools and technologies as a silver bullet. Such is the findings of research conducted by McKinsey Consulting Company as published in *Harvard Business Review* in October 2003. However, in sharp contrast to common beliefs, the research shows that the application of pure information technology (IT) without strategy does not improve productivity. Instead, application of tools without a strategy, in the best cases, maintains a company on par with its current productivity levels as it grows. Along the same lines, the lean production principles used in the Toyota Production System state, "Any system, which has a series of new technologies growing faster than the capacity to detect problems, will invariably fail." Therefore, companies cannot rely on computers to improve their operations if the internal processes do not support the application of the information technology. Without an advance support process designed by the company for the company, these systems fail.

When you purchase a specific software application or IT solution, you buy not only the specific application, but also the business model developed and promoted by the application manufacturer. For example, every estimation system has an underlying business model in which it makes sense to operate. If the company's processes do not match the business model delivered in the estimation program, the company must change the programming or discard portions of the system, either of which may be cost-prohibitive.

Agile companies design their processes prior to committing to program or IT solutions. The selection and use of the tool follows the process—not the other way around.

■ Corporate Memory

You improve enterprise throughput by improving the entire enterprise, not one part or another. The whole organization must become Agile and more productive to translate the Agile benefits into more profits. Chaos and unorganized processes in the company are the direct result of lack of planning and application of structured approaches. The natural state of any system is chaos; it takes work to maintain order. The time, effort, and cost devoted to combating chaos pulls resources and drastically reduces your agility.

Yet a side effect of overlooking process design is a haphazard culture that deals with issues and problems instead of growth and learning. For example:

- Project managers who do not apply time management principles effectively try to use their memory to keep track of issues and resolve a job's process issues and concerns. This approach often creates urgent situations. Eventually, the project manager ends up in a situation in which everything is urgent. However, once everything is urgent, nothing is urgent because every issue has the same weight and therefore no priority.
- Project managers who lack planning and foresight introduce rework as a result of firefighting and applying bandages. They respond expediently to crises in ways that may not address the real issues at hand.
- Project managers who run their jobs without paying attention to increasing the productive time and reducing nonproductive activities expend additional effort on nonproductive activities, which reduces the visibility of the process and worsens the system's time to detect and time to react.

The purpose of pursuing agility is to increase profits by correctly responding and addressing the needs of the job site and company. The most satisfied customer is also the most profitable customer. To design the supporting organization for

Agile operations in construction, the company needs to reduce tribal memory and increase corporate memory.

As mentioned previously, several operational models exist for both union and nonunion electrical contractors. The prevailing operational models for all electrical contractors are the following:

- Traditional (technically oriented)
- Transitional (in transition from traditional to professional)
- Professional (business oriented)

Although both union and nonunion electrical contractors are represented within these three operational models, the majority of union and nonunion electrical contractors began as and remain traditional, technically oriented companies. Often, these companies were initially founded on the technical knowledge of the company's leader. Corporate memory resides with this one person, who can complete each job within the company if the need arises.

Transitional electrical contractors, with business processes and procedures that are outlined and specified, arise out of the traditional models, usually when the company has grown to such a size that it is difficult, even impossible, for the company leader to be everywhere at once and to serve as a singular point for all company knowledge. Transitional contractors recognize the necessity and benefits of the professional operational model but have not transitioned entirely.

When the transition is complete, the company operates within a professional operational model, which relies mostly on corporate memory, as depicted in **FIGURE 8–3**, not so much on individual know-how and memory. In the professional operational model, tacit knowledge is translated into explicit knowledge and the flexibility of applying problem-solving methods is expanded to the lowest levels of the company. Professional companies employ the following standardized project management and system design features:

- Strategic planning and marketing plans
- Field feedback
- Seamless material handling and tracking

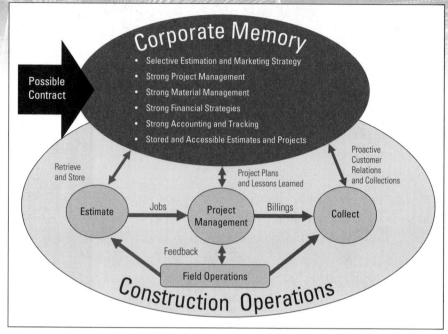

FIGURE 8–3 Professional operational model.

- Increased estimation accuracy
- Standardized project management
- Business visibility

Most everything you use to do daily tasks was designed and produced by a human. Every day you deal with numerous products to accomplish work. We simply assume that it has to be that way, since without design and development; we would have no tools or equipment to help improve our quality of life. However, when it comes to processes that rely heavily on human interaction, most believe that the processes can happen by themselves. This chapter introduces the principles and tools you can use to design processes based on sound and time-tested management science. Like everything else in the world of business, the processes that you design can be useful and functional only when you integrate the interaction with the user into the design. Just as hardware design takes into account human–machine interaction and ergonomics, Agile design requires input and consideration of the user.

Processes

Processes exist in all businesses, whether they are defined, documented, visible, and agreed upon, or they simply evolve as a part of the prevailing culture. Well-defined processes streamline the relationships between individuals and functional areas of the organization.

A *process* is a collection of steps and procedures that creates a deliverable. It starts with an objective and ends with a deliverable and should be designed to be self-correcting. A *procedure* is the series of activities necessary to complete each step of the process.

The procedures in an Agile company must support the processes without restricting responsiveness. Much like the process defines the inner workings and flow of information and work, procedures define how and when work and information are expected to flow throughout the organization.

Many contractors initiate their approach to Agile Construction™ by focusing on procedures: by reviewing and revising current procedure manuals, policy manuals, and training documentation. They look at the consistency and correctness of their procedural steps, where to find or keep project documentation, who receives certain reports, how to place a material order.

Process versus Procedure

The main difference between a procedure and a process is that the steps of a procedure do not require validation whereas the steps of process do. A process may raise such questions as, "Why are we doing this?" or "Where does this add value?" You can answer these questions only at the process level.

A procedure concentrates on correctness of the step and tries to improve its efficiency. Processes constantly question the necessity of every step and work on the effectiveness of events. According to MCA research, the average electrical contractor spends $42 on internally processing every purchase order (PO). In other words, a $3 switch box costs the company $45, before the cost of receiving and installation. By evaluating each procedural step in the purchase order process, you can concentrate on the correctness of individual steps without considering the total cost of processing. When considering the PO process, on the other hand, you ask questions such as follows:

- Do we need this many POs?
- Can we work with one PO per vendor?
- Can we use Electronic Data Interchange (EDI) instead?

To put it simply, the procedure works on "doing the things right," whereas the process works on "doing the right things." Correct procedures improve efficiency and correct processes improve effectiveness.

Four processes lie at the core of an Agile company:

- Strategic Breakthrough Process Improvement (SBPI)
- Process of project management (POPM)
- Process of procurement (POP)
- Process of estimation (POE)

Each of these processes plays a critical role in the management of a project as well as in the feedback loop that develops and supports the learning culture that enables the company to make ongoing improvements.

Of course, every project must include all of the activities contained in the processes and all individual activities must be performed to complete the project. Every project requires a schedule of values, manpower planning, timesheet tracking, billing, material ordering, and many other activities. What makes a contractor Agile is not the completion of the activities, but rather the design and implementation of a consistent process that binds together the activities to achieve a predictable result.

Each step in the process must be designed to that step's own specifications and needs. Just as in an automobile, if an engine part doesn't meet specifications, the performance of the engine subsystem is unpredictable. Further, if the performance of the engine subsystem is unpredictable, the performance of the entire vehicle is unlikely to meet customer expectations. The same is true for construction projects: If the elements of the process of procurement, for example, are not designed to predetermined specifications, the procurement process will yield unpredictable results and the likelihood that the project is completed on the customer's schedule and on budget is very slim.

Strategic Breakthrough Process Improvement

An organization cannot immediately stop its current operations to apply Agile Construction techniques at once. Strategic Breakthrough Process Improvement (SBPI) enables an operating contractor to apply the principles of Agile operations in manageable sections without losing sight of the overall transformation.

By systemically applying the four phases and eight deliverables of the SBPI process, an organization can transform itself into a near perfect delivery system for products and services.

The four phases of implementation are the following:

1. Identification
2. Characterization
3. Optimization
4. Utilization

Each phase supports two major deliverable activities, as shown in **FIGURE 9–1** and discussed in subsequent sections. Together they provide a structure for first identifying the areas of the organization that contain opportunities for improvement, and then characterizing those issues for optimizing within the system. By using learning tools (such as Plan-Do-Study-Act cycles) and operational measurement and process control tools (such as JPAC®), you can build a learning organization that engages in continuous study and improvement through designed processes and control points and ultimately uses standardized

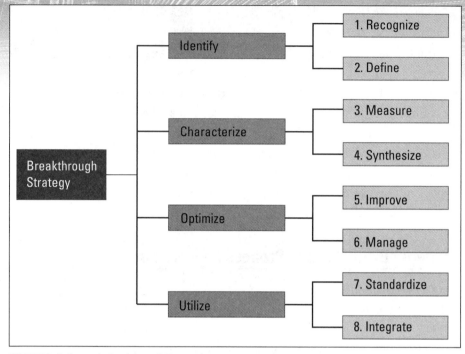

FIGURE 9–1 Strategic Breakthrough Process Improvement outline.

processes and improvement strategies throughout. (See Figure 9–1 and **FIGURE 9–2**.)

Identify: Recognize and Define

Recognition of performance shortcomings as they relate to the customer's expectations is the very first step in the application of Agile processes. The identification stage of SBPI focuses on diagnosis of the issues affecting system productivity and throughput by recognizing the situation and defining the scope:

- What are the issues?
- What are the opportunities?
- How do they manifest?
- Which areas are involved?
- How extensively?

True issues and waste in the company are often hidden; that which appears to be the issue is frequently no more than an effect from a different problem entirely. For example, the labor may complain about lack of material availability on a certain

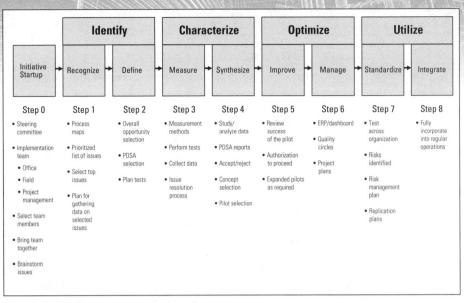

FIGURE 9–2 SBPI with detailed activities within each step.

day; however, the true root cause of their complaint may be that they were forced to do an unscheduled task. If they could have conducted their work as planned, they would not have been short of material. The true cause of material shortage in this case is the lack of access to the planned work area. For this reason, a clear definition of the problem is essential.

In addition, many issues affect multiple areas of the organization in a variety of ways. The issue that is the hottest topic for the warehouse may barely show up on the radar in estimating or accounting. You must prioritize issues systemically to identify those areas that are strategically misaligned with the overall vision of the company, and without exception, you must recognize the impact of each issue on the customer. In addition, in the prioritization recognize each issue's potential impact on profitability, productivity, and resource availability.

By understanding the most significant cause (in a broad sense), whether it suggests process, personnel, tools, material, or the physical setting is the underlying cause, you can direct energy and effort to that issue.

To recognize the true roots of issues, processes must be made visible and you must understand all connections and interactions. The best approach to showing the connections is to develop a spaghetti chart (see Appendix C) that clearly identifies every function involved in a particular process and the communication network between them (**FIGURE 9–3**). Among the concerns that the spaghetti chart highlights are the following:

- Multiple functions repeating the same activity
- Back and forth interaction between two areas
- One-way communication channels (dead-ends)
- Significant communication routed through one functional position

From there, a deployment flow (see Appendix C) mapping the current process can help to identify bottlenecks, convolutions in the process, excessive departures from a streamlined flow, process ownership, and other impediments to agility.

Once you have made visible the causes of rework, waste, and errors and understand their impact on other areas of the company, the cross-functional team can develop a focused plan to target the systemic issues with full knowledge of the inter-departmental effects. For example, a change in the warehouse can easily require a change in the order entry system, whether intentional or not.

Plan-Do-Study-Act (PDSA) cycles begin at this stage with a clearly defined statement of the issue and a proposed plan to target it. (See Appendix D.)

Characterize: Measure and Synthesize

A critical part of the implementation of Agile is verification of improvement resulting from process redesign. The characterization stage of the SBPI initiative brings in measurements and analysis, seeking to validate the issues. Are they real or perceived? How big is the opportunity for improvement in terms of capability, throughput, productivity, or cost? What is the potential financial impact?

An essential component of the PDSA plan must be to develop how and where the problem will be objectively measured. All improvements come through change, but by no means is every change an improvement; proposed process revisions must

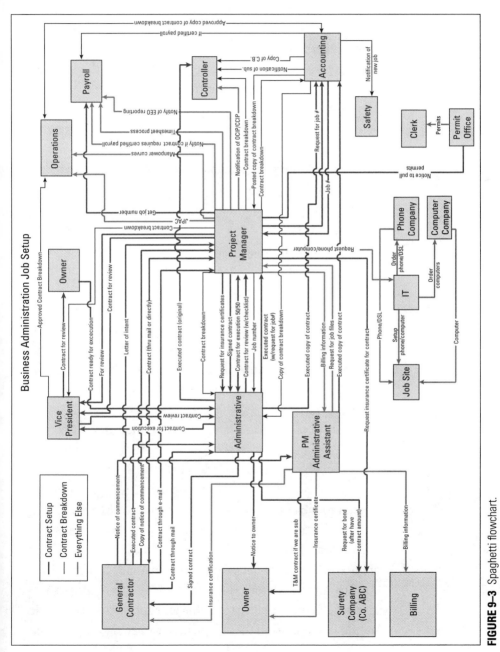

FIGURE 9-3 Spaghetti flowchart.

prove themselves on a small scale before you expand or adopt them unilaterally.

In many cases, the initial problem is identified on a "gut feel" level—it seems difficult, unwieldy, complicated, or excessive. For example, for a large project with 80 electricians onsite every day, the lack of productivity may be hard to identify. The general foreman has a gut feel that something is wrong. In a comparable real case, once the JPAC showed a dip in productivity, MCA conducted a workshop with all the foremen and electricians to brainstorm the root cause of the problem. The answer unanimously was excessive time spent on material receiving and handling. Based on this response, the general foreman hired seven unindentured electricians to work for an experienced foreman to manage the material handling. The job's productivity increased by more than 30 percent. Many contractors' instincts are correct; however, they must be tied to measurements to provide a gauge by which to judge proposed changes. Some processes lend themselves to many different measures; successive PDSA cycles can focus on improving these one at a time until a test has fully been proven.

Although PDSA cycles are designed to be run in quick, short increments, it is very important to recognize that the test is being run in an artificial environment. The people carrying out a new procedure not only need time to learn the new procedure; in many cases, they must test the new one without giving up the old. It may make for extra work in the short term. The first set of measures might show an increase in resource usage as people adjust before stabilizing to the improvement level after the learning cycle has been further developed or completed. Additionally, to expedite the PDSA cycle, it is important to include those who are most affected by the changes in the redesign process. Their input ensures their buy-in later for full-scale implementation and they know intimate details about the procedure and adjustments that may be needed.

The intention, however, is to keep the PDSA cycles short term and focused. For example, the initiators of the PDSA cycle should find out first if the information gathered on a proposed new purchase order form really is the correct and required information before they apply system resources to fully develop the infrastructure and process for using the form. The initial PDSA cycles are learning tools. The concept must be proven first: You must consider whether you are doing the right thing before you consider whether you are doing it correctly. Take data in context because raw numbers can be misleading, especially in seasonal or cyclical businesses.

Application of PDSA to test hunches, gut feelings, and points of distress in the workflow very often disprove those subjective expectations. It is not unusual to see failure in 25 to 50 percent of the tests, which by itself is an important tool for verifying an inappropriate hunch for the applied process. The failure of a PDSA is in reality not a failure of the test, but rather the disproving of the initial hunch. At a large electrical contractor in Kansas City, the purchasing department believed that their material return refunds could be increased if they had a better policy. During the PDSA, it was discovered that on an annual basis, the material return was less than 1 percent of the annual sales. The time spent on managing the return of the material was in excess of 5 percent. The project was abandoned. This hunch failed; however, they discovered that they could save money by reducing the labor cost of the material handling by working with their distributors to return the material during the progress of the job. They adopted the return-as-you-go process. Another organization with a different process goal, philosophy, and operating structure might very well have higher material return than labor and accept the same exact test as a successful improvement. It is critical for the whole organization to be aware of the potential failure rate. If the organization believes it will be perfect without failure, the desire to continue to implement change will lose momentum and upper management support.

Moreover, the analysis of any test results needs to be made with a conscientious awareness of the Hawthorne effect. This is a phenomenon that occurs when people are observed during a research study and, as a result of the observation rather than of the test, temporarily change their behavior or performance. The effect is named for the Hawthorne Works, where one study in a series of experiments on factory workers investigated the effect of lighting on workers' productivity. Researchers found that productivity almost always increased after a change in illumination, no matter what the level of illumination was, leading to the conclusion that the experience of participating in a test affected the results.

To avoid the Hawthorne effect, select and institutionalize only the significant changes that lead to lasting improvements. For this, you have to design and implement a change-management process, which will control the versions of process and procedure and will reduce the confusion of which form or procedure is the latest and most current. This process is identified in the SBPI (Strategic Breakthrough Process Initiative).

Optimize: Improve and Manage

The optimization stage of SBPI is one of the most critical stages in the application of Agile because it includes designing for improved management of the changed processes.

After proposed changes have been tested, you select the successful major elements and pull them together into a unified pilot design. At this point, you put the concept under stress: Can it withstand full-scale operations? Do negative effects appear or overwhelm the system with additional volume? A test that showed promise on a small scale may need additional support or infrastructure before you can implement it on a larger scale. For example, at an electrical contracting company in northern New Jersey, an initial PDSA proved the concept of the cost code usages in a few projects to be useful for job tracking. The cost codes were then agreed upon and were used across a large number of jobs as a pilot. Testing the cost code concept under real and multiple project conditions identified usage issues the contractor did not see before doing the PDSA. One of the main issues in this case was the semantics of the cost codes. The new users of the cost codes interpreted them differently. Therefore, the labor-hour and productivity allocation to the cost codes became erroneous. During this pilot run, the contractor addressed these issues, and prior to full implementation, they developed a user's manual to explain the cost codes.

Once a concept has been proven on a small scale, successful tests are put under stress in larger pilots before you implement a major redesign of the process. This additional testing phase sets the stage for a successful implementation of redesigned processes.

You can define, test, and carry out the pilot plan using the same process as the original PDSA: begin with defining the expected result, a specific description of the pilot and its parameters (who is involved, when, how long, etc.), the measurements that will be used to evaluate the pilot, and the criteria to judge its success.

If the pilot is a success, the cross-functional team needs approval from management to implement the change across the organization. The authorization request is supported by documentation done at each step of the PDSA cycles and pilot tests, showing a demonstrable effect on the bottom line.

Support processes are not an important consideration in the testing phase. However, once the pilot has proven itself and has been approved for implementation, it can only be expanded on if it has been designed correctly with the appropriate support. The implementation design should include new process maps to show the flow and structure of the proposed implementation. Earlier maps showed "current state." At this point, you can introduce logic flowcharts to make the new design visible, including the underlying structure and how to address exceptions.

The expansion plan for the pilot must also include the communication plan for the new design. How will you communicate the change? What information must be shared? In what format? The testing team is often in full support of the change initiatives because they understand the development of the pilot and can predict the ripple effects. They also have the background knowledge of the test results and how the new procedure affected each area. In other words, their own hesitations have been addressed. Resistance to change becomes a critical factor in implementation; the rest of the organization must come to the same level of understanding through training, education, and well-founded trust that poor concepts have been eliminated prior to implementation. If you do not communicate the plan effectively, achieving buy-in and understanding from all involved, implementation may still fail even if the pilot was successful. In the previous example of cost code implementation during the pilot, the contractor discovered an additional issue—the resistance of a few foremen to reporting their timesheet and productivity measures for JPAC progress. It took four workshop sessions and evidence-based training to convince these foremen to cooperate. Their resistance to change was not malicious; they simply wanted to be trained in it and see their fingerprints on the process.

Unlike the test and development phases of new processes for Agile, full implementation and application across the organization require much more rigidity and structure. You must also continually measure progress.

Because many companies use a multifaceted approach to identify and target the major waste and causes of rework simultaneously, they can use a visible dashboard or Enterprise Resource Planning (ERP) system to ensure that changes and measurements are visible and can be easily monitored. The dashboard or ERP system should show all critical measures of the system.

FIGURE 9–4 shows a sample of the dashboard concept. At a minimum, the dashboard should include the following:

- Definition or description of each measure
- Scope of the measure
- Graphics—charts or tables (with clear descriptions and labels)
- Target performance levels
- Measurement "owner" (who keeps and updates the data)
- Last update or revision date
- Data collection and reporting cycles

	Revenue	Gross Profit	Operating Profit
Company Performance			
	JPAC	SIS	WIP
Project Performance			
	AR Aging	Cash Flow	AP Aging
Financial Performance			
	Pipeline	Backlog	Hit Ratio
Estimation Performance			

FIGURE 9–4 Sample company dashboard.

You can also use project plans to track the pilot and actual implementation of the new design. The plan again serves as visible means of communicating the scope and outcome of the project as well as manageable tasks, a schedule, and reported progress.

All mechanical, electrical, and biological products require some kind of maintenance to operate optimally and continuously. The best kind of maintenance is not generally repair, rather preventive care. Processes are not much different from physical systems; they require constant maintenance to operate at optimal output. A quality circle (QC), which is a structured approach to continuous learning and maintenance of a system, has to be created. The members of the QC are people who are familiar with the process and can solve the problem and issues immediately.

The institutionalization of Agile processes carries unique risks. If you do not manage the process correctly, any of the following can turn into a major pitfall during the implementation phase:

- Management support
- Management understanding

- Available resources
- Correct training
- Personnel shifts
- Lack of buy-in
- Mismatch of risk or rewards with the new process

Risk management must be an integral part of the overall approach to change management, so risk identification must be part of the implementation plan. By carefully managing to reduce the unknown or uncertain elements and increase the known facts of the situation, you can mitigate risk if not avoid it. Requiring constant feedback from all stakeholders—customers, vendors, management, production workers, salespeople, back office personnel—is one method of effectively reducing the risks. To this end, use an efficient issue resolution process to capture and address all problems arising as a result of the new design. For example, a large electrical contractor in Atlanta, Georgia, reduced material management risk by creating a vendor-managed inventory partnership with two of their suppliers. They reduced the number of vendors from 77 to 2. The process the contractor used, described on page 180, was to create the statement of work and select the top contenders. They reduced the risk of material management by placing inside sales personnel from the two distributors on site at the contractor's office. They conducted weekly meetings between the distributor, project managers, and field foremen to improve communication. They developed an issue resolution form and process to capture all the material-related mishaps and needs, which the appropriate department then dealt with immediately. This process helped all the participating parties to benefit from better communication and reduce their cost of operations.

Utilize: Standardize and Integrate

Overall recognition and acceptance of the new process comes only when the results speak for themselves and do not need any interpretation. Designed changes are sustainable only when they are fully incorporated. Agile must become a part of daily business.

The next step in SBPI is to institutionalize the concepts by making change management an enterprise-wide strategy focused on learning and translating that into sustainable improvements in terms of time, cost, and quality. The SBPI process and the fact-based learning culture it supports must constantly and consistently run in the background of the entire system.

■ Process of Project Management

The second critical Agile process is the Process of Project Management (POPM). Your agility as an electrical contractor is strengthened by employing a standardized process of project management. Every time you hire a new electrician, there is a learning curve. Lack of standardized project management practices throughout the electrical contracting industry forces rotating electricians to relearn project management styles and systems with each contractor, each foreman, each GC, and sometimes even each project.

Agile companies are not limited to the knowledge of a single stakeholder. They tend to involve several departments in their project planning and value engineering; often, project managers, foremen, and electricians all have input into estimation. As discussed earlier, Agile companies cross the boundaries between various departments in the company and involve the field, project managers, and office staff in perpetual value engineering. By including more departments in more processes, Agile contractors reemphasize the structured communication flow as well as the wide communication bandwidth.

The process of project management overlays all project-related activities. By standardizing the process of project management, you can flatten the learning curve of any new or replacement resource you add to the project team.

FIGURE 9–5 depicts the logical steps in a common process of project management. Each of the eight steps falls under the segments that define the level of emphasis of management's attention. The three categories and the related activities under them are described in the following subsections.

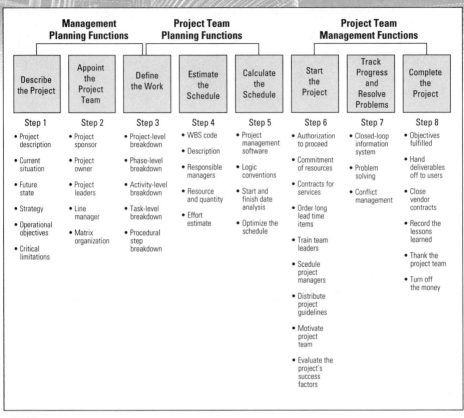

FIGURE 9–5 Process of project management.

Management Planning Functions

In this phase of the process, you should focus on how to standardize the planning part of the project and establish metrics for measuring participation and consistency. All the steps in the process of project management are generic and common among all projects large and small. The process of project management starts with describing the project.

Describe the Project

The project description should be a very simple "elevator piece" (something that can be read and understood in an elevator ride) that describes the project in a very simple form, which could include the following key points of information:

- Project name
- Description

- Current situation—what is known and unknown
- Project completion objective
- Strategy—how the project will be completed
- Operational objectives—any and all milestones or deliverables
- Assumptions and risks—general behaviors and other potential issues

Next, you must appoint the project team.

Appoint the Project Team

Use this step simply to standardize the process of team selection. Evaluate how management selects the project team. What are the required characteristics of the personnel for the specific project on hand? A checklist can help. For example, a midsize electrical contractor in Buffalo, New York, created a checklist that identified the type of job, such as hospital, commercial, or industrial. They then looked into the project management and foremen experience and created the team needed for the type of project. Because the nature of every contractor's business varies, you must create the project team selection list based on the company's experience and exposure to various types of projects.

Next, you define the work.

Define the Work

You need to identify both the project-related work and supporting work of the office, prefabrication, warehouse, and/or any other department. At this stage, the breakdown and definition of work for various departments and people allows the project team to work with clear and defined responsibilities and authorities for go-to people.

Project Team Planning Functions

The project teams, which include associates representing all the functions that support the project, begin planning for project start-up. The team reviews the project's technical, financial, and integration risk, identify action items, and then select responsible persons for solving and reducing project risk. To do this the project team should complete the following three steps.

Define the Work

The team uses the work that was defined in the previous phase and adds the resources, time, and deliverables to clarify the steps needed to create the project delivery schedule.

Estimate the Schedule

In addition to the job-related scheduled plan, the project team should identify and estimate the schedule for every department and activity that supports the project.

Calculate the Schedule

Based on the estimated schedule developed in the previous step, the project team can create the actual project delivery schedule, calculated and optimized for the best usage of the resources. It is of utmost importance that the optimization of the schedule is based on resource capability and availability and does not allow the time to be the element that defines the importance of the scheduled tasks. In other words, do not allow procrastination to be the reason for misuse or untimely usage of resources.

Project Team Management Functions

In this part of the process of project management, the measurement metrics become much more resource based than in the previous steps, which rely on checklists and yes-no answers. The metrics can rely primarily on the tools introduced throughout this book for managing the Agile company. At this stage, project delivery focuses on the following three steps.

Start the Project

The project team should notify all parties and departments involved in project delivery that the project is about to start. The team can create a shared space where they can post the project's information to help eliminate any communication issues and misunderstandings that may arise. The project kick-off meeting should discuss the following topics:

- Activity checklist for all the departments.
- Standing meeting. This is a weekly meeting with a standard agenda that reviews all the relevant weekly events.

- Shared space medium. This describes where all the documents and information about the job can be posted for access by all participants.

Track the Progress and Resolve Problems

Project audits, monthly financial updates, work in progress (WIP), project schedule, three-week scheduled plan, JPAC, SIS™ are all the tools you need to track, correct, and project the job's progress. All participants in the project delivery system should receive the portions of the tools that affect their work. With visible tracking of the project, the measurement tools act as the shared space for information dissemination, prediction, and problem resolution.

Complete the Project

The project team should celebrate the completion of the project. All the resource inflow should be closed liens, and invoices should be taken care of. Any other open issues should be closed. **BOX 9–1** shows a checklist for project closeout developed by Thompson Electric in Sioux City, Iowa.

BOX 9–1 Sample Checklist for Project Closeout

- Agree on terms
  - As-builts
  - Warranties/guarantees
  - Inspections/walk-throughs
  - Software
  - Start-up
  - Spare parts
  - Testing
  - Punch list sign-off
  - Training
  - Transfer utilities to owner
- Billing complete
- Retention returned
- Material returned
- Equipment returned
- Tools returned
- Bonds released
- Liens released
- Change orders invoiced
- Job records archived
- Customer satisfaction survey complete
- Utility disconnects
- Occupancy permits
- Accounting close out (last day of labor/ liens required)

■ Process of Procurement

The third Agile process arises from the need to step beyond the internal control of the company to the essential interaction with suppliers to coordinate and procure the material needed to complete the project.

Integrating Agile Construction techniques into the supply chain requires a specifically designed and carefully implemented process of procurement. Although applications certainly vary from one company to another, effective application of an Agile procurement process requires consideration of each of the following six elements (see also **FIGURE 9–6**):

- Procurement planning
- Procurement scheduling

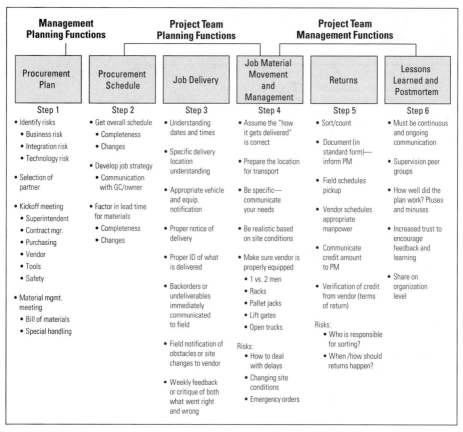

FIGURE 9–6 Process of procurement.

- Material delivery
- Job site material storage and movement
- Returns
- Lessons learned

Procurement Plan

The procurement plan should include identification and communication of the various risks associated with the project, and specifically with the material aspects of the project.

Three primary categories of risk are associated with material procurement:

- *Business risk.* Business risk is associated with material pricing or price fluctuation, the cost of vendor services vs. handling and storage at the contractor's site, and the cost of warranty and contractor commitment to service issues. Business risk may also include consideration of liquidated damages and open-ended performance contract terms.
- *Technical risk.* Technical risk is associated with the accuracy of the take-off, the completeness of the system and its design, the correctness of the material, the proper function of the installed components, and compliance with code, specification, and submittal. Technical risk may also include consideration of alternates that were proposed at the time bid but not yet approved for use.
- *Integration risk.* Integration risk is associated with the movement of material, installation methods and techniques, productivity and trade coordination, communication on the job site, proper tracking of materials, maintenance of the inventories, and job site safety.

Although the procurement plan identifies the various risks associated with any given project, the planning step rarely contains details relating to how the risk will be mitigated. This is for very good reason: The procurement plan can, and should, be developed by the contractor; however, each of the stakeholders has an interest and a unique ability to contribute to mitigating the various risks. Steps 2 through 5 all contain various solutions to overcome the identified risks; these solutions are developed jointly by the supply chain participants for the specific construction project.

Because the specific stakeholders all contribute to the development of steps 2 through 5, the final event in step 1 is the selection of supplier partners.

Procurement Scheduling

The Agile contractor does not wait for the installers to request material before considering how to get it there. Just as the supplier must be able to recoup the costs of providing services, the supplier also needs time to provide those services. If you plan to benefit from supplier services, you have to coordinate with the supplier to allocate sufficient time to prepare the material and coordinate the delivery as requested. Agile contractors do not rely on suppliers to provide 7:00 a.m. deliveries when they place their orders at 3:00 p.m. the previous day; next-day deliveries do not contribute to Agile results.

Scheduling should account for lead times for engineering, manufacturing, shipment, preassembly, and verification, staging, and specific constraints associated with job site delivery dates and times. Often overlooked in the procurement scheduling function is a detailed consideration of time buffers. Knowing who owns the buffers and how they are visible and shared among the stakeholders can greatly improve the agility of the entire construction effort.

When shipping damage is detected, what are the contingencies for correction? These issues cannot just flow down to the job site and become the installer's concern; procurement planning and scheduling anticipate possible failures and provide means for early detection and correction of any errors, before they reach the job site.

The procurement schedule is a living document; it must be maintained, current, and accurate to be useful for construction. Construction project schedules are constantly changing, and this affects the various buffers you have planned into the schedule. You need to identify the owner of the logistics management tasks and ensure that these are maintained. (See **FIGURE 9–7** for a sample procurement schedule.)

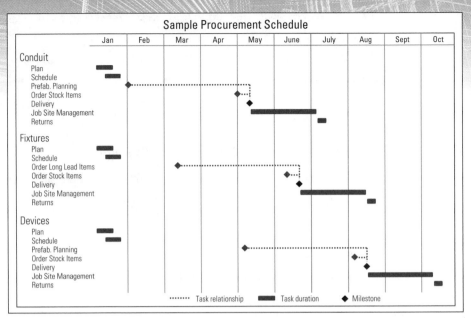

FIGURE 9–7 Sample procurement schedule.

Material Delivery to the Job Site

In step 1, the plan identifies who will make the deliveries. In step 2, the schedule identifies when the deliveries will be made. In step 3, the details of how the material will be packaged, labeled, loaded, and unloaded are coordinated. If you do not plan these decisions in advance and leave them to chance on the day of delivery, the installers will face unplanned interruptions and certain loss of productivity.

In some cases, you need to plan and coordinate material deliveries for each specific "drop"; in other cases, you can develop an efficient routine for commodity items delivered on a regular basis. Routine deliveries are a good practice for packaged items that are delivered in specific quantities to specific areas and for prefabricated or preassembled components that are going to specific locations at specific times. Less-routine deliveries may be planned for large equipment drops and deliveries that require coordination with specialized handling equipment.

Regardless of whether each delivery is a uniquely planned event or a recurring event, the packaging, labeling, and handling should all be consistent and exactly as planned. In many cases, the best results are achieved when the same supplier sends the same driver in the same truck to any given job site. Although this practice seems unnecessarily restrictive, the cost associated with, for example, a covered truck when the job site personnel are expecting an open flatbed can be unrecoverable. (See sample delivery packages in **FIGURE 9–8**.)

Job Site Material Movement and Storage

There are several considerations with regard to material storage locations on the job site. Perhaps the most important factor is recognizing that any time installers are moving material, they are not installing material. MCA's studies have shown that as much as 40 percent of the labor's time on any job is spent handling material; this is not contributing to Agile Construction.

Material that is prepared for installation and delivered to the point of installation at the time of installation is the most beneficial and predictable means of material movement. Making one drop in the final location is very efficient; however, it is not always achievable. In some areas, job site layout doesn't permit material deliveries in this fashion; in other areas labor agreements do not support this type of material movement. Maximizing labor installation efficiency is the key to Agile Construction. When material must be stored on

FIGURE 9–8 Sample delivery packages prepared by a distributor.

the job site, then storing it in a location where it is protected from damage and will not need to be moved unnecessarily is always best.

Ensure that wherever the material is stored it is labeled with what it is, where it came from, and where it will be installed. Record when the material was received, who received it, and who inspected it. Minimizing the delivery locations is not nearly as desirable as minimizing the movement, distance, and frequency. You must also consider the capability of suppliers in the area where material is delivered directly to the work site. Not all suppliers can provide such services because many lack the safety qualifications, delivery means, and manpower to deliver material directly to the work area.

You should plan on-site material inventory as a buffer. The buffer should be rational and logical to support changes that are beyond the control and anticipation of the installers. However, excessive material buffers are costly and unnecessary. Inventory represents a significant investment of cash, labor, facilities, and equipment for all businesses, including contractors.

By increasing job site inventory, you do not decrease the risk of productivity loss; you simply shift the risk away from too little material. Risk of work stoppage as a result of inadequate quantity of material is replaced by increased risk of work stoppage resulting from incorrect material and excessive material handling. Traditional efforts, such as consigned inventory, have done little to reduce the cost of large job site inventory; instead, they accomplish little more than shifting the burden and expense from the contractor to the supplier.

Historically, contractors have allowed field supervisors and project managers to determine and purchase the necessary material types and quantities required for their projects without providing specific material management or procurement logistics training and education to these employees. Without adequate training, field supervision maintains an inventory level that provides a personal degree of comfort. Often this is based on past experience with the vendor or with material shortages from underestimation of the consumption rate. In fact, it is a very common practice for contractors to purchase and ship as much as 80 percent of the anticipated material to a job site at the time of initial mobilization. This is very costly and hinders the ability of installers to continue uninterrupted installation.

Carrying too much job site inventory and keeping it too long results in another avoidable cost for contractors: the high cost of unnecessary material returns. The opposite is also true— carrying too little job site inventory and ordering it too late result in unproductive labor and unplanned work being executed. There is a fine balance between too much and too little job site inventory. An Agile contractor must constantly review and monitor job site inventory to keep up with changing job conditions.

Material Returns

Many contractors demand that suppliers take back material, often without restocking charges, and perhaps they even request full credit for their leftover material. This practice is costly to the entire supply chain and only drives future material costs higher.

Usually, there are very good reasons for material returns, and sometimes they are beyond the control of the contractor. The most common reasons for material returns include the following:

- Incorrect material was ordered.
- Incorrect material was shipped.
- Changes to the plan require different material.
- Material was not needed; too much material was maintained for comfort.
- There is inadequate space to store the material.
- Delivery time did not occur when specified.
- There was no way to handle the material as shipped.

Because material returns are a cost for everyone in the supply chain and a benefit to no one, anything that you can do to reduce or eliminate the unnecessary manufacture, shipping, delivery, receipt, storage, handling, tracking, and accounting associated with material improves your agility.

By forming a partnership with the supplier to manage the material on the job site, you can help reduce material returns. The following supplier services are beneficial for both partners:

- On-site trailer
- Vendor gang box management
- Vendor return management

    (See also Figures 6–14 and 6–15 in Chapter 6.)

Lessons Learned

Capturing lessons learned is the most important contributor to Agile procurement. Without effectively capturing which practices are beneficial and which practices are not, you cannot maintain any Agile benefits on future jobs. A postmortem review of procurement should focus on each step in the process of procurement. At a high level, the factors that lead to sustainable improvement are related to application of the following fundamental principles and concepts:

- Prejob planning
- Job schedules
- Delivery schedules
- Value engineering
- Job site material management
- Return and damage control

■ Process of Estimation

Estimation is the lifeline of any contractor. It is the engine that drives sales and the development of new work. Without it, you cannot get work, sustain the size of your company, or compete. Often, however, the process of estimation in many electrical contracting companies is not visible. Agile contractors use a visible process of estimation (POE) that feeds forward the assumptions made at the estimation stage into the organization and feeds back the company's and field's capabilities to marketing and sales.

Before you develop an internal estimation process, you must build a marketing and project selection process to identify the projects that you will bid on. Agile companies approach the market recognizing what the market can offer. Regardless of the project or contract type (that is, whether the project is hard-bid, design-build, cost-plus, guaranteed-maximum-pricing, or time and material) each potential project has to go through a visible selection process. **FIGURE 9–9** shows a simple process of project selection. Out of the available work, each project must be evaluated as to whether its size and duration fit the company's core competencies. By examining the purposes and risks associated with pursuing (or not pursuing) particular projects, you can reduce the choices to a short list using a decision matrix or estimation filter such as the one shown in **FIGURE 9–10**. (For a more detailed estimation filter, see Appendix D, Figure D–5.)

With agility, you can pursue even more jobs. The risk is reduced as more information becomes available to you about

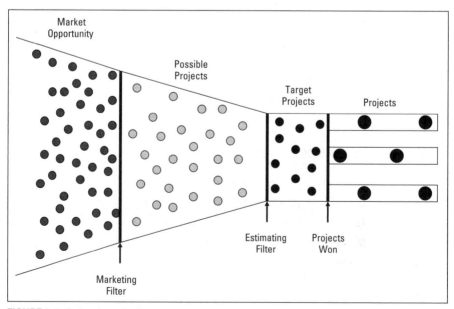

FIGURE 9–9 Estimation selection process.

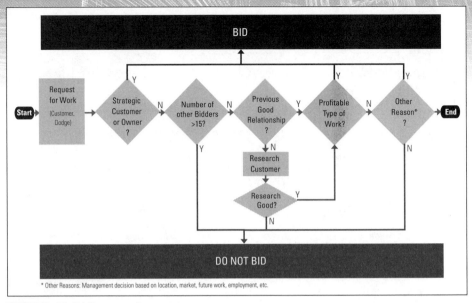

FIGURE 9–10 Bid filter example.

how that type of work or different work with similar characteristics and conditions is worked in the field.

Once you have identified a potential project and have evaluated the risks associated with it, the internal process of estimation starts. The generic steps of the process of estimation are shown in **FIGURE 9–11**. The eight steps of POE are categorized in three segments that define the level of emphasis of management's attention. The three categories and the related activities are described in the following subsections.

Identification

In this phase of the process of estimation, you should focus on how to identify potential jobs. You can use an estimation filter, such as the one shown in Figure 9–9, to determine potential projects.

Identify Opportunities

Following are opportunities where jobs can come from:

- Existing customers
- New customers
- Service work

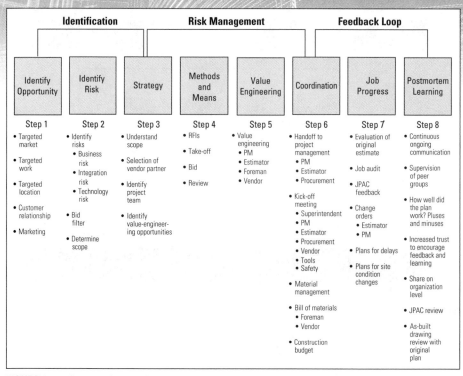

FIGURE 9–11 Process of estimation.

- New type of work
- Social activities and engagements
- Philanthropic involvements

Identify the Project Risks

Every project with electrical work also comes with risk. The following risks are involved:

- *Technical risk:* Do we have the know-how?
- *Business risk:* Can we make money? Can we cash-flow the job?
- *Integration risk:* Can we have manpower, tools, and material come together for an efficient installation?

Risk Management

Once a project meets the first cut, it is brought into the estimating department. The estimation team has to work on their plan to mitigate any potential risk that the project will have. Assuming that there is enough estimation capability, the reduction of risk requires input from various departments throughout the company. The following four steps mitigate risk.

Strategy

A risk mitigation strategy includes a clear, step-by-step assignment for each department that supports the project's installation.

Methods and Means

You must identify, document, and track all the means and methods that will be used to mitigate the risk.

Value Engineering

Every estimate should offer an alternative solution to the owner, which proves the expertise of the contractor to the owner. The value engineering at this stage could simply include an alternative installation method to reduce the cost.

Coordination

Estimation is a relatively costly process for contractors. MCA's data show that the national average hit ratio (dollars bid vs. dollars won) is only about 10 percent. The cost contribution of the estimation to the contractor's overhead is around 1 percent of dollars bid. To avoid costly reestimation by project managers or foremen, coordination with and passing on of the assumptions to the project team are very critical in the POE.

Feedback Loop

The estimation analysis section of the book (EAE™) explains in detail the feedback loop needed to increase estimation accuracy. The POE requires a clear and visible procedure to help improve estimation accuracy. The following three steps are necessary in the feedback loop.

Coordination

Estimation coordination with the project management and field labor is the most critical portion of the POE in regard to gathering accurate data. JPAC and SIS based on common cost codes can supply the most accurate feedback through a well-designed coordination procedure.

Job Progress Report

Use financial, JPAC, WIP, and SIS reports to inform estimation about the correctness of project progress. Additionally, project audits give the estimators collective feedback on job progress and help improve the labor units used to estimate the jobs.

Lessons Learned and Captured

Like all the other Agile processes, estimation ends with capturing the lessons learned. This is where all the processes begin, end, and come back together.

■ Conclusion

Procedures standardize the activities that are commonly used throughout companies and organizations. By themselves they are neither wrong nor right. Their usage and the involvement of people turn them into processes. Processes can be right or wrong depending on their effect on the company's overall productivity and profitability. Processes must be designed carefully to avoid waste and rework. Processes must take into account required training, measurements, and standardization. Any time the flow of material, information, or work is interrupted, there exists the potential for mistakes, rework, and waste that affects the final outcome of the process. It is of utmost importance that process design accounts for interruptions. For example, a foreman fills out the purchase order correctly by following the right procedure, but he fails to inform the appropriate parties about the time of delivery—process failure. Following the correct procedure but not using the right process costs this foreman productivity, and therefore the job loses profitability. Correct procedures increase efficiencies; correct processes improve effectiveness.

Safety Data

Data Collection

Nonfatal Injuries and Illnesses

The Bureau of Labor Statistics reports data on fatal and nonfatal injuries and illnesses by Standard Industrial Classification (SIC) code. This data is collected through the Survey of Occupational Injuries and Illnesses, which is both a state and federal program in which employer's reports are collected annually from about 176,000 private industry establishments and processed by state agencies cooperating with the Bureau of Labor Statistics.[1] Under those guidelines, nonfatal cases are recordable if they are occupational illnesses or if they are occupational injuries that involve lost work time, medical treatment other than first aid, restriction of work or motion, loss of consciousness, or transfer to another job. Employers keep counts of injuries separate from illnesses and also identify for each whether a case involves any days away from work or days of restricted work activity, or both, beyond the day of injury or onset of illness.

To assess the impact of safety in construction, we used data on "Days Away from Work" due to injury or illness. The data are available electronically for 1992 through 2006.[2] An example of the data available is shown in TABLE A–1.

Hours Worked

The Bureau of Labor Statistics collects data through the Current Employment Statistics survey on number of employees and average weekly hours worked by SIC code.[3] These sources were used, along with the following assumptions, to calculate the average annual hours worked in electrical construction by the

TABLE A–1 Sample Data Set from 1992: Days Away from Work Due to Nonfatal Injuries and Illnesses, by Industry (Report 65)

	SIC	TOTAL	Number of Cases per Category of Days Lost						
			1 day	2 days	3–5 days	6–10 days	11–20 days	21–30 days	31 days or more
Construction		209,564	32,099	25,496	40,346	26,564	22,292	14,128	48,639
General building contractors	15	44,632	7,393	5,196	8,662	5,566	4,673	3,195	9,947
Residential building construction	152	20,913	3,504	2,423	4,142	2,502	2,249	1,497	4,596
Operative builders	153	638	88	86	132	52	68	45	166
Nonresidential building construction	154	23,081	3,802	2,687	4,388	3,013	2,356	1,653	5,184
Heavy construction, except building	16	32,255	4,474	3,584	5,868	4,004	3,791	2,040	8,493
Highway and street construction	161	10,628	1,531	1,317	1,894	1,361	1,160	603	2,762
Heavy construction, except highway	162	21,627	2,942	2,266	3,975	2,643	2,631	1,438	5,732
Special trade contractors	17	132,677	20,232	16,716	25,815	16,993	13,828	8,893	30,199
Plumbing, heating, air-conditioning	171	28,397	5,272	3,835	5,480	3,512	2,737	2,022	5,540
Painting and paper hanging	172	6,319	603	779	929	821	615	531	2,041
Electrical work	173	19,471	3,512	2,556	3,561	2,282	2,111	1,175	4,274
Masonry, stonework, and plastering	174	22,211	2,694	2,550	4,565	3,335	2,270	1,324	5,473
Carpentry and floor work	175	9,058	1,444	1,179	1,798	1,188	889	482	2,079
Roofing, siding, and sheet metal work	176	11,872	1,464	1,452	2,101	1,522	1,418	907	3,007

same population of workers on which injuries and illnesses are reported for 1992–2006. Assumptions include the following:

- Data are not seasonally adjusted (seasonal adjustment indicates the adjustment of time series data to eliminate the effect of intrayear variations, which tend to occur during the same period on an annual basis).
- Data represent production workers (nonsupervisory).
- There are 50 working weeks per year.

TABLE A–2 shows sample data for number of production employees, and **TABLE A–3** shows sample data for average weekly hours worked by production workers.

Fatalities

Data on fatalities are kept by the Bureau of Labor Statistics as the Census of Fatal Occupational Injuries (CFOI) by SIC code.[4] The census uses multiple sources to identify, verify, and profile fatal worker injuries. Information about each workplace fatality—occupation and other worker characteristics, equipment involved, and circumstances of the event—is obtained by cross referencing the source records, such as death certificates, workers' compensation reports, and federal and state agency administrative reports. To ensure that fatalities are work-related, cases are substantiated with two or more independent source documents, or a source document and a follow-up questionnaire.

Nature of Injury

The data reported to the Bureau of Labor Statistics on injuries and illnesses include demographic characteristics of the injury or illness, including the following:

- By nature
- By parts of body affected
- By sources
- By events or exposures
- By hours worked before event occurred
- By day of the week event occurred
- By time of day event occurred

TABLE A–2 Number of Production Workers, All Construction

Series Id: CEU2000000006
Not Seasonally Adjusted
Super Sector: Construction
Industry: Construction
NAICS Code: N/A
Data Type: Production Workers, Thousands

Year	Jan	Feb	Mar	Apr	May	Jun	Jul	Aug	Sep	Oct	Nov	Dec	Annual
1992	3186	3100	3181	3393	3596	3718	3794	3843	3791	3788	3667	3492	3546
1993	3185	3200	3236	3475	3740	3884	3996	4044	4006	4016	3923	3740	3704
1994	3419	3368	3508	3796	4025	4182	4292	4327	4303	4274	4197	3986	3973
1995	3658	3585	3718	3946	4127	4305	4395	4438	4414	4408	4289	4072	4113
1996	3740	3773	3882	4127	4353	4529	4639	4679	4645	4638	4545	4350	4325
1997	4009	4036	4140	4361	4592	4736	4850	4885	4842	4829	4723	4549	4546
1998	4258	4255	4303	4606	4818	5002	5132	5169	5096	5115	5031	4896	4807
1999	4530	4584	4641	4933	5133	5321	5435	5441	5387	5388	5333	5132	5105
2000	4870	4825	4991	5164	5326	5498	5593	5604	5530	5523	5416	5204	5295
2001	4920	4921	5044	5199	5408	5567	5640	5625	5544	5513	5389	5214	5332
2002	4908	4883	4934	5066	5234	5392	5438	5447	5383	5349	5265	5055	5196
2003	4729	4661	4741	4946	5157	5326	5391	5421	5381	5354	5268	5095	5123
2004	4804	4761	4909	5121	5338	5508	5609	5629	5568	5599	5518	5340	5309
2005	5026	5039	5160	5432	5637	5821	5891	5944	5890	5919	5898	5679	5611
2006	5464	5484	5587	5792	5995	6139	6194	6236	6129	6081	5957	5778	5903
2007	5537	5409	5587	5739	5951	6142	6187	6167	6081	6050	5912	5662	5869
2008	5363	5301	5356	5463	5627(p)	5751(p)							

(p) = preliminary

TABLE A-3 **Average Weekly Hours Worked, All Construction**

Series Id: CEU2000000007
Not Seasonally Adjusted
Super Sector: Construction
Industry: Construction
NAICS Code: N/A
Data Type: Average Weekly Hours of Production Workers

Year	Jan	Feb	Mar	Apr	May	Jun	Jul	Aug	Sep	Oct	Nov	Dec	Annual
1992	36.7	36.7	37.3	38.2	38.9	38.9	38.9	39.1	37.2	39	37.6	37.3	38
1993	36.2	36.8	37.5	37.8	39.2	39.2	39.5	39.6	38.3	39.3	38.6	38.4	38.4
1994	37.1	36.2	38.1	38.3	39.7	39.6	39.7	39.7	39.9	39.5	38.5	38.8	38.8
1995	37.8	37	38.1	37.7	38.5	39.5	39.9	39.7	39.9	40	38.6	38.1	38.8
1996	36.7	38.2	38.1	38.6	38.8	39.6	39.7	39.8	39.7	39.9	38.8	38.6	38.9
1997	36.5	37.5	38.4	38.8	39.6	39.5	40	49.7	40	39.7	37.9	38.5	38.9
1998	37.4	38	38	38.1	39.3	39.1	40.1	40.1	37.5	39.9	38.5	39.1	38.8
1999	37.8	37.9	37.7	38.6	39.3	39.7	39.8	39.9	38.6	39.9	39.5	38.8	39
2000	38.3	38.6	38.8	39	39.5	39.4	39.9	40.1	40	40.1	38.7	38	39.2
2001	38	37.6	38.3	37.9	39.3	39.3	39.5	39.3	39	38.8	38.6	38.1	38.7
2002	38	37.9	37.8	38.2	38.4	39.1	38.9	39.3	39.3	38.7	37.8	37.6	38.4
2003	37.8	36.3	38.2	37.5	38.8	39	39	39.5	39.1	38.9	38.3	37.4	38.4
2004	37.5	37.2	38.3	37.7	38.7	38.5	39.1	39.1	37.6	38.7	38.2	38.2	38.3
2005	36.8	37	37.8	38.7	38.9	39.2	38.8	39.2	39.4	39.1	39.1	38.1	38.6
2006	38.2	38.1	38.4	38.4	38.8	39.6	39.4	39.9	39.3	39.7	38.8	39.3	39
2007	37.9	37.4	38.7	38.4	39.3	39.7	39.4	39.6	39.5	39.6	39	38.6	39
2008	37.9	37.5	38.5	38.4	38.6(p)	39.4(p)							

(p) = preliminary

We used Series R1 (industries by nature) to review the nature of injuries for the construction and electrical construction industries (see **TABLE A–4** on pages 199 and 200 for example data).

■ Data Analysis

Nonfatal Injuries and Illnesses

The data, as listed in Table A-1, show the number of cases in each category of number of days lost. Each case of an injury or illness is one occurrence for one employee, and the categories are not cumulative. In other words, in 1992, there were 32,099 cases of injury or illness in the entire construction industry that resulted in 1 day of lost work. There were 25,496 cases of injuries/illnesses that lead to 2 days of lost work.

The trend in the number of nonfatal injuries and illnesses for all construction is shown in **FIGURE A–1**. The total number of occurrences has been decreasing. A detailed view of the categories shows that the majority of illnesses and injuries result in more than one month of lost time.

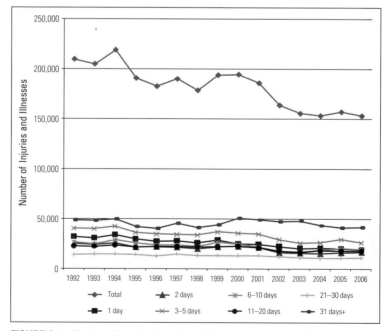

FIGURE A–1 Number of nonfatal injuries and illnesses per year for all construction—total and by days missed.

TABLE A–4 Sample Data for the Nature of Injury or Illnesses, 2006

Industry	NAICS Code	Total Cases	Sprains, Strains	Fractures	Cuts, Punctures	Bruises	Heat Burns	Chemical Burns	Amputations
Other nonmetallic mineral mining and quarrying	21239	150	60	30	—	20	—	—	—
Potash, soda, and borate mineral mining	212391	70	30	—	—	—	—	—	—
Other chemical and fertilizer mineral mining	212393	40	—	—	—	—	—	—	—
All other nonmetallic mineral mining	212399	30	—	—	—	—	—	—	—
Support activities for mining	213	3,950	890	700	200	580	180	30	70
Drilling oil and gas wells	213111	1,360	340	290	110	160	20	20	30
Support activities for oil and gas operations	213112	2,590	540	410	90	420	160	—	40
Construction		153,180	52,880	17,670	23,930	9,460	1,490	1,070	1,220
Construction of buildings	236	29,320	10,520	4,060	4,760	1,560	260	100	440
Residential building construction	2361	16,640	5,410	1,620	3,250	780	190	30	380
Nonresidential building construction	2362	12,680	5,110	2,440	1,510	780	70	70	60
Heavy and civil engineering construction	237	19,400	6,350	2,980	1,470	1,840	190	50	140
Utility system construction	2371	9,010	3,100	1,740	680	720	40	20	50
Water and sewer line related structures construction	23711	5,210	1,690	1,220	380	350	—	20	20
Oil and gas pipeline and related structures construction	23712	920	270	140	70	80	20	—	—

TABLE A–4 Sample Data for the Nature of Injury or Illnesses, 2006 *(Continued)*

Industry	NAICS Code	Total Cases	Sprains, Strains	Fractures	Cuts, Punctures	Bruises	Heat Burns	Chemical Burns	Amputations
Power and communication line and related structures construction	23713	2,880	1,150	380	230	290	—	—	20
Land subdivision	2372	450	120	50	100	20	—	—	—
Highway, street, and bridge construction	2373	7,660	2,590	900	540	930	130	30	80
Other heavy and civil engineering construction	2379	2,270	530	290	160	180	20	—	—
Specialty trade contractors	238	104,460	36,010	10,630	17,700	6,060	1,040	910	640
Foundation, structure, and building exterior contractors	2381	28,820	8,590	3,740	5,200	2,140	450	60	280
Poured concrete foundation and structure contractors	23811	5,240	1,820	690	550	500	—	30	30
Structural steel and precast concrete contractors	23812	2,850	560	580	240	310	20	—	40
Framing contractors	23813	5,410	1,270	580	1,560	460	—	—	80
Masonry contractors	23814	5,900	2,320	830	620	340	—	—	70
Glass and glazing contractors	23815	1,500	480	210	410	50	—	—	20
Roofing contractors	23816	5,620	1,770	640	1,020	280	400	—	30

Because the data are listed by cases in each category, we calculated a weighted average of days lost to determine the impact on labor-hours. The weighted average is calculated as follows:

Weighted Average of Days Lost = (# cases of 1 day × 1)
+ (# cases of 2 days × 2) + (# cases of 3–5 days × 4)
+ (# cases of 6–10 days × 8) + (# cases of 11–20 days × 15)
+ (# cases of 21–30 days × 25) + (# cases 31 or more days × 50)

The weighted average of days lost in 2006 was 2,943,690 days. Assuming an 8-hour workday, this translates to 11,510,850,000 hours lost in 2006 as a result of nonfatal injuries and illnesses.

The SIC codes for construction are in the hierarchy shown in **FIGURE A–2**; the colored boxes highlight the path to electrical construction.

For analysis, we compared electrical construction, building construction, overall construction, and private or all industry.

The trend of hours lost, using the previous method for calculating the weighted average, is shown in **FIGURE A–3**

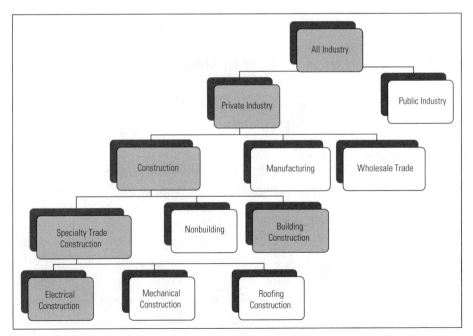

FIGURE A–2 Hierarchy of SIS codes for construction.

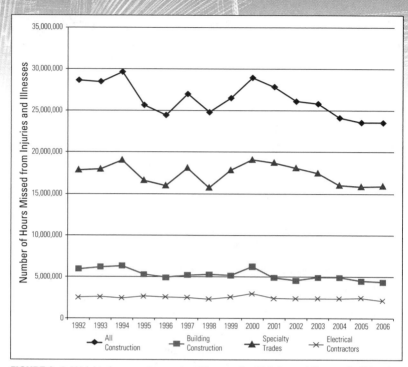

FIGURE A–3 Weighted average hours missed from nonfatal injuries and illnesses by SIC code.

for all construction, building construction, and electrical construction.

Specialty trades result in more days lost than building and nonbuilding construction. **FIGURE A–4** shows a pie chart of the 2006 hours missed for each component.

To further weight the impact of the lost time, we compared the lost hours to the calculated hours worked in each industry. The calculation of hours worked is this:

Hours Worked = Number of Production Workers
× Average Weekly Hours Worked × 50 weeks/year

FIGURE A–5 shows the trend of lost time from nonfatal injuries and illnesses as a portion of the total time worked per year, according to the preceding calculations. Trend lines show the decrease in lost time as a portion of hours worked in all represented industries; however, based on the equations of the trend lines, the slope of the all construction injury trend is decreasing faster than that of all industries and electrical construction.

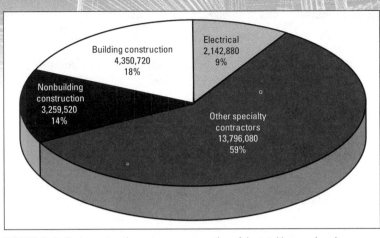

FIGURE A–4 Each construction category as a portion of the total hours missed as a result of nonfatal injuries and illnesses in 2006.

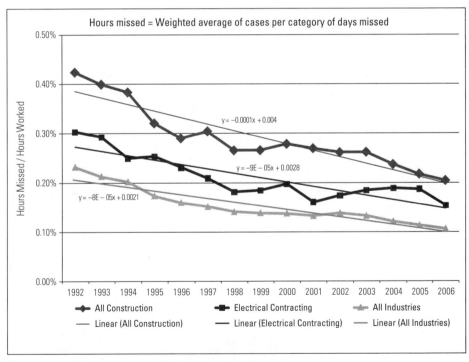

FIGURE A–5 Hours lost as a result of nonfatal injury and illness as percentage of hours worked in all construction, electrical contracting, and all industries.

The number of nonfatal injuries and illnesses per million workers is shown in **FIGURE A–6** by industry category. The number of workers is based on the Bureau of Labor Statistics data for production workers.

Fatalities

The trend of fatalities in the construction industry is shown in **FIGURE A–7**, for overall construction, building construction, and electrical subcontracting.

The number of fatalities and nonfatal injuries and illnesses is shown for electrical as a portion of building construction in **FIGURE A–8**, electrical as a portion of all construction in **FIGURE A–9**, and all construction as a portion of all industries in **FIGURE A–10**. The vertical axis is scaled differently in Figure A–8 than in Figures A–9 and A–10 because electrical incidents

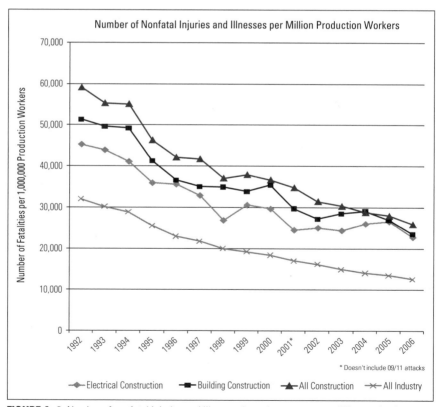

FIGURE A–6 Number of nonfatal injuries and illnesses in each category, per million production workers.

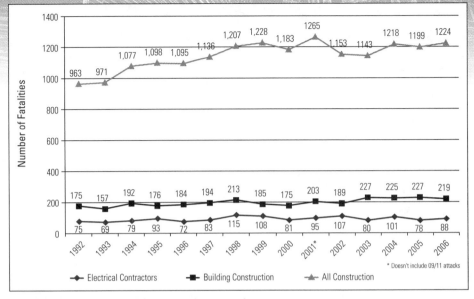

FIGURE A–7 Number of fatalities per year in construction.

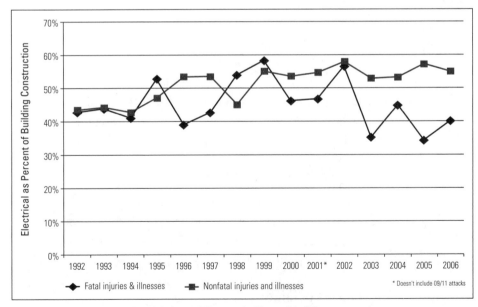

FIGURE A–8 Fatal and nonfatal injuries and illnesses in EC vs. all building construction.

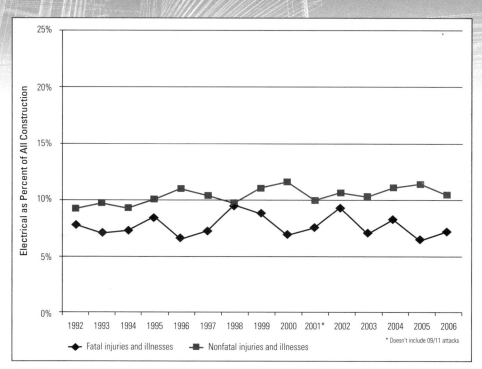

FIGURE A–9 Fatal and nonfatal injuries and illnesses in EC vs. all construction.

are almost 70 percent of the number of incidents that occur in building construction.

Similar to Figure A–6, **FIGURE A–11** shows the fatalities per million production workers. The fatalities per million workers are about 1 percent of the nonfatal injuries and illnesses shown in Figure A–6.

Comparison to Other Industry

FIGURE A–12 shows how the trend of number of nonfatal injuries and illnesses in the construction industry compares to all industries. Construction represents about 13 percent of all injuries and illnesses.

Causes of Injury

FIGURE A–13 shows the nature of illnesses in the construction and electrical construction industries. The chart is ordered from largest to smallest by each category for the electrical construction industry.

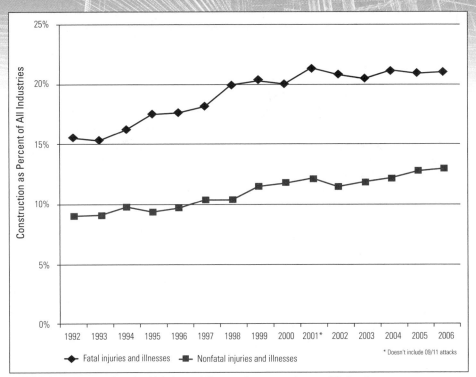

FIGURE A–10 Fatal and nonfatal injuries and illnesses in construction vs. all industries.

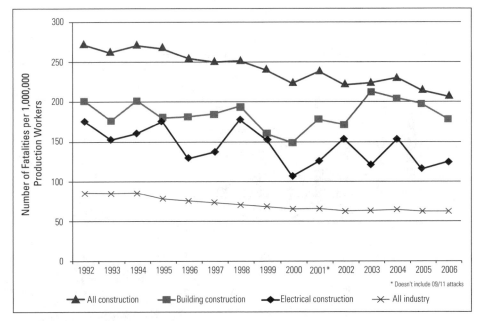

FIGURE A–11 Fatalities per million production workers.

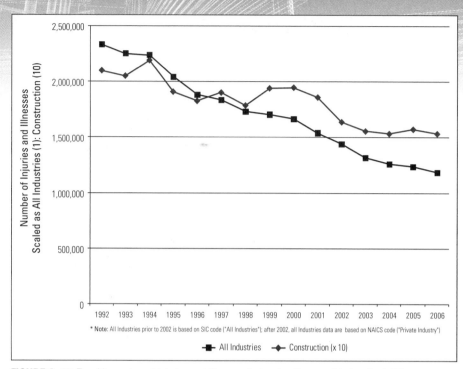

FIGURE A–12 Trend in number of injuries and illnesses in construction vs. all industries (×10).

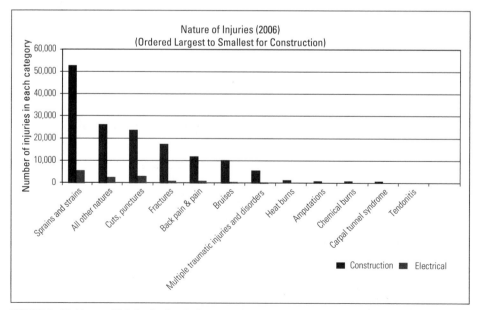

FIGURE A–13 Nature of injuries in electrical construction vs. all construction.

■ References

1. Bureau of Labor and Statistics, "Injuries, Illnesses, and Fatalities: Occupational Safety and Health Summary Data," February 5, 2002, http://data.bls.gov/cgi-bin/print.pl/iif/oshsum1.htm (accessed June 3, 2009).
2. Bureau of Labor and Statistics, "Detailed Industry by Number of Days Away from Work (Table R65)," http://stats.bls.gov/iif/oshwc/osh/case/ostb2007.pdf (accessed June 3, 2009).
3. Bureau of Labor and Statistics, "Current Employment Statistics," http://www.bls.gov/ces/home.htm (accessed June 3, 2009).
4. Bureau of Labor and Statistics, "Census of Fatal Occupational Injuries," http://www.bls.gov/iif/oshcfoi1.htm (accessed June 3, 2009).

Plan-Do-Study-Act Cycles

Every improvement in an organization comes from a change, but not every change is an improvement. Plan-Do-Study-Act (PDSA) is a learning process that provides a structure for testing changes on a small scale prior to implementing them company-wide. If a suggested change fails in implementation, it is much more expensive than if it fails in a test environment. The PDSA process involves short cycles in which changes are tested incrementally, and the change is either discarded or improved until it proves to be beneficial.

You can develop PDSA topics once the current system has been made visible, using process mapping, data collection, and cause-and-effect analysis. Once you answer the initial questions, a group of people come together to start the cycle. The group can include the users of the process being studied, experts in the process being studied, data collectors from the process, and outsiders who are not involved in any way with the process. This Plan phase of PDSA should answer the following questions about the suggested change:

- What are we trying to accomplish with this change?
- What is the impact of this change on the overall organization?
- How will we know that change is an improvement?
- How will we measure the improvement?
- What change are we going to test? (Be specific about what change to test, who will test it, how long the test will last.)
- What are the expected results of the test (counts, measures, observations)?
- How will the results be measured?

- How will the measurements be analyzed?
- What is the plan for the next PDSA cycle? What will we be trying to learn in our next iteration? What does the company want to learn from the PDSA cycle?

Once the test has been defined and planned, the Do stage of the cycle is where the testing occurs. During the test, the group can ask the following questions:

- Was the test performed as planned? (If not, why not?)
- What data were collected and what observations were made?

The results of the test do not always match the expectations. During the test, the productivity may worsen, but that does not mean it is time to abandon the test.

Once the test is performed, the group studies the results to evaluate the gap between expected results and actual results. The data collected during the test are compared to the base line to measure the change. The questions to answer in this step are the following:

- Were the results of the test what we expected? (Compare this answer to the questions answered in the planning phase.)
- What do the data tell us about the change? (What changed both within the process being tested and in any other processes impacted?)
- Is the change an improvement?

Once the results have been evaluated, the group must decide to accept or reject the change. If the test was successful (even if the expected results were not achieved), the group can develop additional tests to further test the potential change. Sometimes several iterations of PDSA are needed to achieve the expected or desired results. In the Act stage of PDSA, the group asks the following questions:

- Is the change accepted or rejected?
- Is further testing needed, or can the change be piloted company-wide?
- What are the specific next steps or action items?

PDSA FORM
(For Testing a Change Aimed at Improvement)

Project/Task Name:

Line Item from Project Plan or Action Item List:

Team Name—Team Leader:

Task Leader:

What is the overall work of the project trying to accomplish?

What is the purpose of this PDSA Cycle— what do you intend to learn?

How will you know that a change is an improvement?

PLAN—Plan a change/test aimed at improvement. Details of the plan:

• Describe the change to be tested (who, what, when—how long, where, how, etc.)

• Results you expect to produce

If we do this (specific action), then we will get this result (specific results in units of measure, counts, observations, answers to questions, etc.)

• How will the results be measured?

• How will the results be studied and evaluated?

• What will the next PDSA cycle be designed to learn?

FIGURE B–1 Plan-Do-Study-Act form.

• What was learned in the entire PDSA cycle? Can this be applied to any other processes?

FIGURE B–1 shows a form that includes the questions to ask at each stage of the PDSA cycle. For more information and further study of PDSA cycles, consult the work of Walter A. Shewhart, listed in the References and Resources section.

Process Mapping

Process maps and workflow diagrams are pictorial presentations that clarify the way in which a process or activities work, singly or together. When used to examine existing processes and activities, they can help identify unnecessary complexity, wasteful, or redundant activities within existing processes as well as help to examine the origins and results of additional workflow steps. They can also be used to design and fully develop new or improved processes.

Although there are many different forms of flowcharts, among the most useful in the application of Lean processes are these:

- Spaghetti chart
- Deployment flow

The initial step of process design is mapping the existing processes to gain a thorough understanding of how things work for the company today. The most effective way of understanding current processes as well as designing new processes is to use time-tested mapping and flowcharting techniques. Mapping is not limited to processes; you can show the flow of authority, communications, and work through the organization by using a variety of flowcharts including logic flowcharts, deployment flowcharts, and time-based flowcharts. The spaghetti and deployment flowcharts are the focus here because they are the most helpful in Agile Construction™.

Spaghetti flowcharts, or information flowcharts, are a good starting point for understanding the functions involved in a process and the information or communication exchanged between the functions. The first step in creating the spaghetti flowchart is to identify the scope of the process. This flowchart does not show the start and end terminator steps of the process. Next, define the functions involved in the process (not the individuals' names, but the positions they represent) at hand and list them on the chart in boxes. Place the main functions involved in the process near the middle of the chart (see **FIGURE C–1**, where the Estimator is in the middle, as the focal point of the estimating process).

Once the process scope and functions are identified, draw the lines of communication from one function to another. The lines of communication represent any information or communication passed, either verbal (such as a phone call, question, or notification) or tangible (such as an e-mail message, document, or visible signal). The arrows are always one-directional because the communications can happen only one at a time.

You can use deployment flowcharting to show the flow of work in a process between the functions involved. It combines the functions involved on the spaghetti flowchart with the sequencing of the steps and decisions in the process. Create a deployment flowchart by listing all of the functions involved with the process along the horizontal axis at the top of the page. Next, draw a "swim lane" vertically below each function on the page. List the steps involved with the process along the vertical axis.

For each step, place a flowchart symbol in the swim lane of the function that performs the step. **FIGURE C–2** shows the symbols used in deployment flowcharting, and **FIGURE C–3** shows an example of a deployment flowchart. Demonstrate processing steps, decisions, wait or delay, and so forth.

When you create the deployment flowchart, it is critical to ensure the chart represents the as-is process, not the process as it should be or as it is documented. It is also important to identify and think through all of the potential decision points along the process made by each of the functions. Finally, make sure all of the loops in the chart are "closed." This means that no step should end without an arrow coming out of it, unless it is a terminator or reference to a separate process.

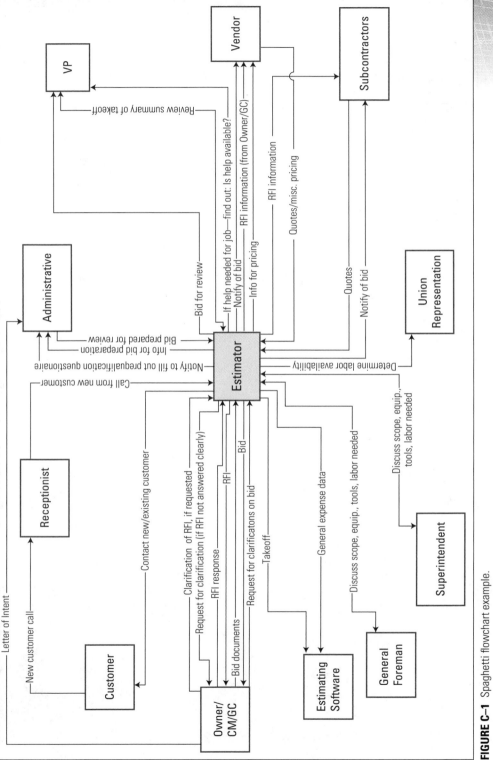

FIGURE C–1 Spaghetti flowchart example.

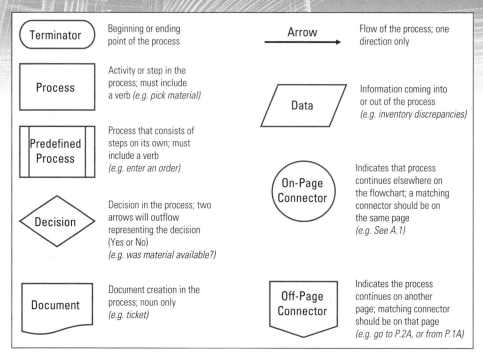

FIGURE C–2 Flowcharting symbols.

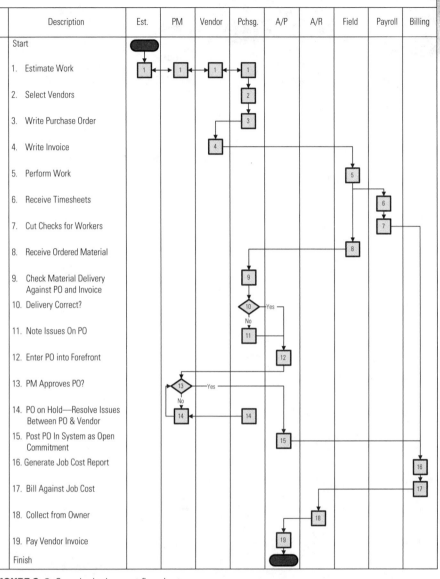

FIGURE C–3 Sample deployment flowchart.

Job Planning and Estimation Flowchart

It of outmost importance that every job prior to starting go through a planning and layout. Planning a project starts with the work breakdown structure (WBS). In this appendix examples of the four phases of the project work breakdown structure are illustrated. Additionally an example of the estimation filter for job selection is shown as a reference for estimation process design help.

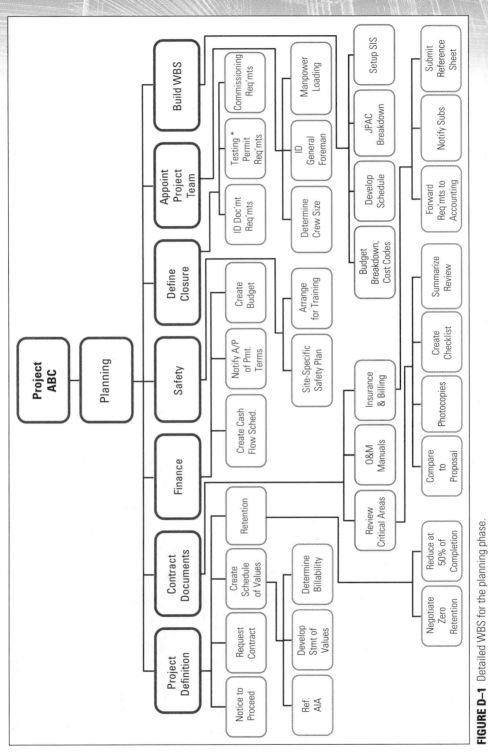

FIGURE D–1 Detailed WBS for the planning phase.

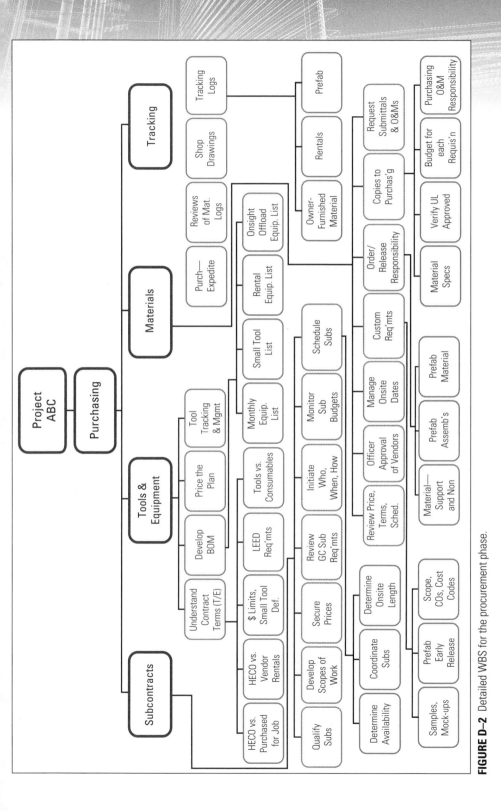

FIGURE D–2 Detailed WBS for the procurement phase.

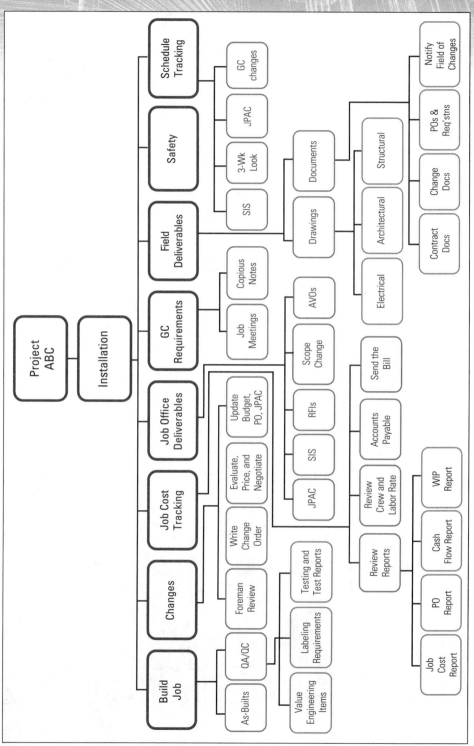

FIGURE D-3 Detailed WBS for the installation phase.

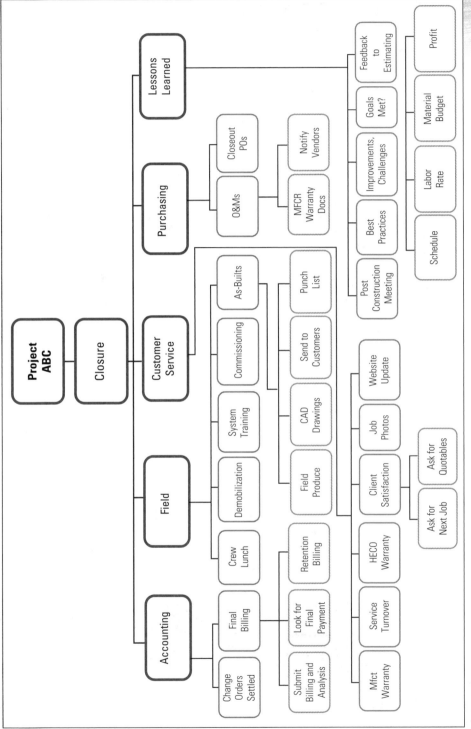

FIGURE D–4 Detailed WBS for the closure phase.

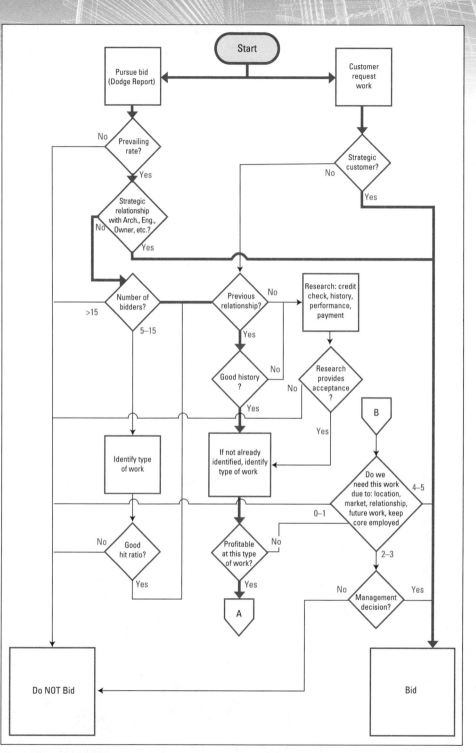

FIGURE D–5 Sample detailed estimation filter.

References and Resources

References

Perry Daneshgari and M. Wilson, *The Impact of Variation on Electrical Contracting Profitability* (Bethesda, MD: ELECTRI International, 2006).

Perry Daneshgari and P. Nimmo IV, *Ideal Jobsite Inventory Levels to Improve Profitability* (Bethesda, MD: Electrical Contracting Foundation, 2008).

Perry Daneshgari and S. Harbin, *Procurement Chain Management in the Construction Industry* (Bethesda, MD: Electrical Contracting Foundation, 2004).

Perry Daneshgari, *A Comparison of Operational Cost of Union vs. Non-union Electrical Contractors* (Bethesda, MD: Electrical Contracting Foundation, 2004).

Perry Daneshgari, *A Strategy for Improving the Electrical Contracting Industry* (Bethesda, MD: Electrical Contracting Foundation, 2006).

Perry Daneshgari, H. White, and M. Wilson, *Developing a Format for Calculating Market Share* (Bethesda, MD: ELECTRI International, 2008).

Perry Daneshgari, H. White, and M. Wilson, *We Build This City* (Bethesda, MD: ELECTRI International, 2008).

Perry Daneshgari, *Lean Distribution in Wholesale Distribution* (Washington, DC: National Association of Wholesalers Institute for Distribution Excellence, 2008).

Perry Daneshgari, *Optimized Operational Model for Maximizing Electrical Contractor's Profitability* (Bethesda, MD: Electrical Contracting Foundation, 2002).

Perry Daneshgari, *The Chase* (San Diego, CA: Black Forest Press, 1998).

Perry Daneshgari, *Wireless Technology and the Electrical Contractor* (Bethesda, MD: Electrical Contracting Foundation, 2002).

■ Resources

American Society for Testing and Materials, "Job Productivity Measurement," (standard practice, pending Fall 2009).

Chris Argyris, *On Organizational Learning* (Cambridge, MA: Blackwell Publishers, 1993).

Damon Schechter and Gordon Sander. *Delivering the Goods* (Hoboken, NJ: John Wiley, 2002).

Diana Farrell, "The *Real* New Economy," *Harvard Business Review*, October 2003.

Ed Rigsbee, *Partner Shift* (New York: John Wiley, 2000).

Eugene F. Brigham, *Fundamentals of Financial Management*, 5th ed. (Orlando, FL: Dryden Press, 1989).

Fredrick Taylor, *Principles of Scientific Management* (New York: Harper & Brothers, 1911).

Gregory Clark, *A Farewell to Alms: A Brief Economic History of the World*, (Princeton, NJ: Princeton University Press, 2007).

James Swartz, *The Hunters and the Hunted* (Portland, OR: Productivity Press, 1994).

John Nash, *Essays on Game Theory* (Williston, VT: Edward Elgar Publishing, 1996).

Kevin P. McCormack, William C. Johnson, and William T. Walker, *Supply Chain Networks and Business Process Orientation, Advanced Strategies and Best Practices* (Boca Raton, FL: CRC Press, 2003).

M. Kotabe, X. Martin, and H. Domoto, "Gaining from Vertical Partnerships: Knowledge Transfer Relationship Duration and Supplier Performance Improvement in the U.S. and Japanese Automotive Industries," *Strategic Management Journal* 24, no. 4 (April 2003): 293.

Parviz (Perry) Daneshgari and Gene Dennis, "Inventory Management Through Supplier Partnership" (presentation, National Electrical Contractors Association, Las Vegas, NV, 1998).

Parviz (Perry) Daneshgari, Mike Romanowski, and Thomas Stimson, *Application of QFD Correlation Matrix Technology to Engine Development Time* (Warrendale, PA: Society of Automotive Engineers, 1996).

Ronald Moen, Thomas W. Nolan, and Lloyd P. Provost, *Improving Quality Through Planned Experimentation* (New York, NY: McGraw-Hill, 1991).

Shigeo Shingo, *A Study of the Toyota Production System from an Industrial Engineering Viewpoint*, trans. Andrew P. Dillon (Norwalk, CT: Productivity, 1989).

Shigeo Shingo, *Non-Stock Production: The Shingo System for Continuous Improvement* (New York: Productivity Press, 2006; original work published 1987).

Shigeo Shingo, *Kaizen and the Art of Creative Thinking*, ed. Tracy S. Epley, Collin McLoughlin, and Norman Bodek (Bellingham, WA: Enna Products and PCS, 2007; original work published 1959).

Sunderesh Heragu, *Facilities Design* (Boston: PWS Publishing Company, 1997).

Taiichi Ohno, *Taiichi Ohno's Workplace Management,* trans. Jon Miller (Mukilteo, WA: Gemba Press, 2007).

Taiichi Ohno, *Toyota Production System: Beyond Large-Scale Production* (New York: Productivity Press, 1988).

Tatsuhiko Yoshimura, *Mizenboushi Method* (Tokyo, Japan: JUSE Press, 2002).

W. A. Shewhart, *Economic Control of Quality of Manufactured Product* (Chelsea, MI: ASQ Quality Press, 1923).

Index

Note: *b* = box; *f* = figure; *t* = table

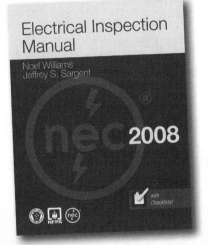